Teach
Yourself

Improve Your Study Skills
Bernice Walmsley

For UK order enquiries: please contact:
Bookpoint Ltd, 130 Milton Park, Abingdon, Oxon OX14 4SB.
Telephone: +44 (0) 1235 827720. Fax: +44 (0) 1235 400454.
Lines are open 09.00–17.00, Monday to Saturday, with a 24-hour
message answering service. Details about our titles and how to order
are available at www.teachyourself.com

For USA order enquiries: please contact McGraw-Hill Customer
Services, PO Box 545, Blacklick, OH 43004-0545, USA.
Telephone: 1-800-722-4726. Fax: 1-614-755-5645.

For Canada order enquiries: please contact
McGraw-Hill Ryerson Ltd,300 Water St, Whitby,
Ontario L1N 9B6, Canada. Telephone: 905 430 5000.
Fax: 905 430 5020.

Long renowned as the authoritative source for self-guided
learning – with more than 50 million copies sold worldwide –
the **Teach Yourself** series includes over 500 titles in the fields of
languages, crafts, hobbies, business, computing and education.

British Library Cataloguing in Publication Data: a catalogue record for
this title is available from the British Library.

Library of Congress Catalog Card Number: on file.

First published in UK 2006 by Hodder Education, part of Hachette UK,
338 Euston Road, London, NW1 3BH.

First published in US 2006 by The McGraw-Hill Companies, Inc.

This edition published 2010.

Previously published as *Teach Yourself Good Study Skills.*

The **Teach Yourself** name is a registered trade mark of Hodder Headline.

Copyright © 2006, 2010 Bernice Walmsley

In UK: All rights reserved. Apart from any permitted use under
UK copyright law, no part of this publication may be reproduced
or transmitted in any form or by any means, electronic or mechanical,
including photocopy, recording, or any information, storage and
retrieval system, without permission in writing from the publisher
or under licence from the Copyright Licensing Agency Limited.
Further details of such licences (for reprographic reproduction)
may be obtained from the Copyright Licensing Agency Limited,
of Saffron House, 6–10 Kirby Street, London EC1N 8TS.

In US: All rights reserved. Except as permitted under the United States
Copyright Act of 1976, no part of this publication may be reproduced
or distributed in any form or by any means, or stored in a database
or retrieval system, without the prior written permission of the publisher.

Typeset by MPS Limited, A Macmillan Company.

Printed in Great Britain for Hodder Education, an Hachette
UK Company, 338 Euston Road, London NW1 3BH,
by CPI Cox & Wyman Ltd, Reading, Berkshire.

The publisher has used its best endeavours to ensure that the
URLs for external websites referred to in this book are correct and
active at the time of going to press. However, the publisher and
the author have no responsibility for the websites and can make no
guarantee that a site will remain live or that the content will remain
relevant, decent or appropriate.

Hachette UK's policy is to use papers that are natural, renewable
and recyclable products and made from wood grown in sustainable
forests. The logging and manufacturing processes are expected to
conform to the environmental regulations of the country of origin.

Impression number   10 9 8 7 6 5 4

Year   2014 2013 2012 2011 2010

> *This book is for all those teachers and tutors who have helped me to enjoy studying throughout my life.*

Acknowledgements

Thank you to the Teach Yourself team at Hodder for their friendly help and guidance. I must also thank my husband William for his continuing support and patience.

Credits

Front cover: © Ryan McVay/Photodisc/Getty Images

Back cover: © Jakub Semeniuk/iStockphoto.com, © Royalty-Free/Corbis, © agencyby/iStockphoto.com, © Andy Cook/iStockphoto.com, © Christopher Ewing/iStockphoto.com, © zebicho – Fotolia.com, © Geoffrey Holman/iStockphoto.com, © Photodisc/Getty Images, © James C. Pruitt/iStockphoto.com, © Mohamed Saber – Fotolia.com

Contents

Meet the author

Welcome to *Improve Your Study Skills*!

With the increasing demand for a flexible workforce many more people are retraining and need to study to improve their career opportunities. However, many people find studying a daunting prospect and don't know where to start. They often believe that they are not capable of obtaining higher qualifications and blame their lack of study skills, thinking that these can't be learned. But they can! And what's more, studying can be an enjoyable experience. With the right approach and a will to acquire the basic skills – such as writing an essay, research and revision techniques, and effective reading – almost anyone can be a successful student, and that is what this book aims to achieve.

Starting with how to get organized, this book takes you through the core skills that will help make studying not only simpler but also more enjoyable. All these skills are dealt with in as straightforward a way as possible, with plenty of examples, tips and insights to guide you in the right direction. So, whether you are a new learner, going back to study after many years or just someone who wants to brush up on a particular skill, this book should be an invaluable tool. By the end of this book, you will have acquired all the essential study skills and have the means to become a successful student!

Bernice Walmsley, 2010

Only got a minute?

Studying is changing. Rather than the strict, regimented approach and the sets of rules and schedules that used to greet anyone starting a new course, increasingly the trend is towards independent learning, giving students more freedom and choice. With this freedom, however, come responsibilities. This means that all students must acquire the skills that will allow them to study successfully and independently. But what are study skills?

Study skills are the techniques, routines and strategies that will make studying any subject easier and more enjoyable. And along the way, many of these skills will also help you in everyday life. Most important among the essential study skills is that of getting organized. If you are a naturally organized person then you will already see the value of having a plan and following it, but if this skill is not one that you have already acquired then be assured that it is a skill like any other and can definitely be learned. Good organization will make studying – and so much else in your life – easier. Much the same can be said of the skill of critically analysing a piece of written work. Learning how to approach academic reading with an analytical mind will change how you read all sorts of things in the future.

Acquiring the necessary skills to become a successful learner will take time and effort but they will become a crucial part of your armoury in the fight to succeed in today's world. Acquiring and practising study skills will help you not only to obtain valuable qualifications but will also give you flexibility in your career and equip you for success in many areas of your life.

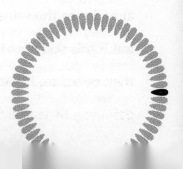

5 Only got five minutes?

There is a widely held belief that you are either good at studying or you aren't. This is not true. Anyone with the desire to learn or to pass an exam can acquire the necessary skills to become a successful student. So, let's look at what these valuable skills are. Top of the list comes organization. Getting organized will ensure that things take less time, you will meet deadlines and you will feel much calmer. It involves making a space for studying and equipping yourself with the things you will need for the task ahead, as well as, of course, planning how you will fit studying into your daily life. Time management, too, is an indispensable skill.

One thing that you will have to do lots of to complete any course is reading. Most of us read on a daily basis but the type of reading you will need to do for academic study is very different. It will involve developing a reading strategy that uses your time effectively; setting goals for your reading (what you need to get from it), asking yourself questions as you read, and assessing the usefulness of what you have learned. You will also need to build up the skills of speed reading and skim reading.

The traditional student activity of note taking is another skill you will have to master. There are different ways to take notes and the method you choose should change according to why you are taking them – do you want them as a simple memory aid or are you making them as preparation for an essay? Keeping your notes organized and accessible is another part of the skill of note taking. Learning how to use the library and the Internet are another two key research skills. You will need to use these skills in a focused way so that you know how much research is needed and always keep in mind your goals. Working in groups is another skill that may be necessary in many courses and which will also be useful in everyday life. For example, a tutor may request a collaborative piece of work, and many students choose to work together for support.

Improving your writing skills will help to make producing any assignment much easier and will give you a much greater chance of passing your course. Apart from acquiring the necessary technical skills such as punctuation, spelling, grammar and readability, the best way to improve your writing is by thoughtful preparation – through a careful analysis of the essay question and thorough planning of your answer.

Exam taking is a skill in itself and one where many students feel they are deficient. But, as always, it is a skill that can be developed if the motivation is there. It is important to remember that examinations are not simply a test of memory, but rather an assessment of your knowledge and ability to think. As ever, organization and preparation are the keys to success.

Finally, in this quick summary of the essential study skills, we should highlight the use of technology. Becoming proficient with word processing and spreadsheet software on a computer can save many hours of work and will result in your work being – and looking! – far more professional.

Acquiring good study skills is a crucial part of successful study, but the good news is that, with patience and dedication, they all be learned!

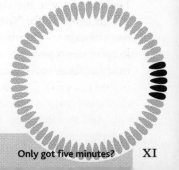

10 Only got ten minutes?

As an independent learner – something we are all being encouraged to be these days – it is your responsibility not only to ensure that you master the basic study skills and use them to your advantage but also to monitor your own progress as a student. It is important that you are aware of what progress you have made and of what further improvements are possible. You may find that the need for the skills you have acquired changes from time to time as you go further in your studies, dealing with ever more complex ideas. You may notice, for example, that the note-taking techniques that you learned and were happy with in the initial stages of your course now seem oversimplified and need some adjustment to capture the more involved concepts that you're now encountering.

For this reason, it is important not to be complacent. Don't think that once you can take notes or write an essay that gets a pass mark you know it all and have acquired all the study skills you will ever need. Yes, you may have mastered some study skills but continual improvement is usually necessary. Could your essays be better? Are there techniques you can learn that will make your essays easier or quicker to write? Or maybe the revision methods you used in the first year of your course or in one subject area will not be quite so perfect in the final year of your course or for a completely different subject area. Acquiring study skills is an evolving process – and one that never really finishes – and this book should prove an invaluable tool to which you can return again and again as you progress through your studies. You'll be surprised how many of the points raised in this book that seem irrelevant to you in the initial stages of your course will become crucial later on. Of course, if you are really stuck on something, you shouldn't hesitate to ask for help from your tutor or counsellor at college or university, but as a first port of call *Improve Your Study Skills* is indispensable.

Continual improvement is something that you should take with you into your working life. If you enter work in a commercial business or in public service you will find that change is constant, as there is a continual push for increased profit, better working methods, reduced costs and increased efficiency. Getting into that way of thinking during your studies will not only enhance your approach to your studies but will also stand you in good stead in your career. Becoming responsible for your own development and aware of the need for change and continual improvement will be knowledge that you can use in interviews and in any job. Many employees are resistant to change and can cause many problems for their employers – don't be one of them! – and make sure that prospective employers know that you have always taken responsibility for your own development, from your college or university days on. Here are some of the study skills, working methods, attitudes and aptitudes that should stand you in good stead throughout your career:

▶ Reading, writing, researching and group working – these are all core skills that are transferable to the workplace and which you will have to use throughout your working life.
▶ Managing yourself – another essential skill in the workplace that you will need throughout your life, evidence for which should be included in your CV.
▶ Organization – applied to your studies, this skill will make things go smoother, improve your results and save you untold amounts of time. Applied to your working life, it will give you exactly the same benefits. Take an organized approach to job-seeking, to your work and, indeed, to your life in general and you will see improvements in every area.
▶ Meeting deadlines – a valuable skill in any career.
▶ A work ethic – simply turning up on time to lectures and getting work done for your course is proof of this.
▶ A desire to get results.
▶ Developing a strategy to get results – showing that you planned what you wanted to achieve and how you wanted to achieve it and that you then worked towards these goals is something that will go down very well with prospective employers.
▶ Identifying your own training needs – if you can see which study skills you need during your studies, then you will probably be able to assess those that you need to do your job.

And who knows, one day you may need to be able to assess someone else's training needs, too, and put a plan into action to help them achieve their goals.

▶ Evaluation skills – being able to evaluate your own needs and what needs to be done to achieve results is essential.

▶ Monitoring your own progress – evidence of knowing just where you are in relation to your plans for your course is useful.

▶ Appreciation of change and the reasons for it – change is constant in business today and people who can embrace change and who also know how to achieve it will find themselves welcomed by employers. Being resistant to change can make working life very uncomfortable, not just for you but also for your colleagues around you.

Consider all these skills carefully and, as you come to the end of your course and begin to look for opportunities to begin your working life, use what you have learned to further your progress in interviews and, then, in your daily working life. Start by including some of these attributes in your CV, giving examples where possible and appropriate. As always, you should tailor what you put in your CV to the requirements of the job for which you are applying.

At the end of your course you may feel that you never want to see another textbook in your life and that, with a new qualification under your belt, you have no further need for learning. You should certainly have a break from intensive studying but don't make the mistake of giving up learning for ever. The other trend today, in tandem with independent learning, is 'lifelong learning'. You may well find that you need to acquire new skills in your new job or to expand the ones you already have. Many employers expect their employees to commit to a programme of continued personal development (CPD). Take all your chances – training and learning is never wasted. And, in any case, with the right study skills, you won't find such opportunities daunting!

Lifelong learning has become essential because of the rapid technological changes that have occurred in recent years – and are continuing to occur at a phenomenal rate. You have to make sure that your skills are continually updated to keep up with the requirements of the workplace and of society in general. In addition, there has been a move towards career mobility and this, too, requires you to develop new skills if you are not to be left behind. Previous generations usually expected to choose, and to train for, one particular career and then that would be what they would do for the rest of their working life. Now it is more than likely that, either out of choice or because of changing economic and social conditions, you will have to to retrain for something completely different after perhaps a few years in a job.

Whatever the circumstances, the study skills that you have learned early on in your student life will prove invaluable. You will probably have to develop them and change them to suit the requirements of your current situation, but the basic principles – getting organized, structuring essays and reports, research techniques and working in groups, for example – will stay pretty much the same. Acquiring good study skills should therefore be high up on the list of any student's priorities.

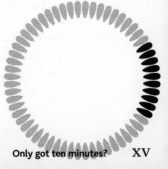

1

Introduction

In this chapter you will learn:
- *how you can use this book to develop your study skills*
- *how you can gain more confidence*
- *how positive thinking can help you*.

Who should read this book?

Perhaps you are following a university course. Or maybe you're aiming at a one-off event such as the written portion of the driving test or a work-based seminar. Or maybe you're trying to gain a work-based qualification such as a national vocational qualification (NVQ) where your competence is assessed 'on the job'. Anyone who needs to learn, in short, can gain from some – or all – of the tips and ideas contained in this book. However, it will be especially useful for those people who are often referred to as 'mature students' and those people approaching independent study for the first time. This would include both new learners and returning learners. It will be useful to anyone who has had difficulties in focusing on their studies in the past or who has no idea where to start with a new course.

In many cases, students will be starting out on a new path in their lives and will need some guidance along the way. If you're a first-year undergraduate or have not studied for some time, you may be surprised by how independent in your studies you will be expected to be. If you've been at school up until this point in your studies, or if your last experience of studying was some time ago, you will find that, although help and support will be available to you, you will need to find out a lot of things for yourself and develop your own way through your studies. Everyone will find slightly different ways to study and will choose their own path, using their own combination of study skills, tools and aptitudes. This book is designed to help you to develop the skills and tools you need to study effectively and to enable you to find, develop and use your own blend of aptitudes to ensure that you are successful in your studies.

How to use this book

This book can be used in a number of ways. You could decide that you are going to improve all areas of your study skills before you start your course and are prepared to sit down and read this book from cover to cover. Alternatively, you could already have noticed a particular area or two of weakness in your study skills and for this you will be able to dip into the book for the appropriate chapters to help you out. You might also choose to keep this book by you as you go through your course, using it as you come up against particular problems.

One thing to remember is that you will not become an expert student overnight. The process of learning study skills must be taken at a speed to suit you – your existing level of skills, your priorities, your current commitments. You may be able to spare the time and effort to read straight through this book in one sitting but this will not mean you have mastered all the study skills discussed. This takes time and plenty of practice, as you will need to try them out on the different types of assignment you're tackling to see how you can use them best.

To use this book effectively, you will need to become familiar with the layout. Check out the contents list now. You'll see that each chapter deals with one broad area of study skills – there's a chapter on note taking, for instance, and one on effective reading.

If you know that you have problems in any of these specific areas, then this will help you to focus on them quickly and easily. Next, if you flick quickly through the chapters, you will see that they all open with a short section starting 'In this chapter you will learn' followed by a few bullet points giving a summary of the expected learning outcomes. This tells you where you can expect to be if you use the information contained in that chapter. This is followed by fairly short sections on all the topics contained in the subject being dealt with in the chapter. This helps in two ways – first, it breaks the information down into more easily digestible chunks and, second, it gives you sub-headings that you can skim through and then focus in on the particular information that you need.

At the end of each chapter you will find three sections – a summary, a quick revision test and a section entitled '10 things to remember'. The summary can be used both as quick revision of what you have learned during the chapter (and, of course, if you see something in the summary that you think you've not really got to grips with, you can then go back and read that section again) or as an outline of what you can expect to find in the chapter before you read it. The '10 things to remember' will help you focus on the key points that you will need to take away from the chapter and apply to your real-life studies. In addition, throughout the chapters you will find quizzes and questionnaires to help you assess your skills and aptitudes as well as plenty of tips to help you save time and effort in your studies.

What are study skills? Can they be learned?

Many students fail to do as well as they are capable of doing because they lack the vital skills that will help them to learn. They are capable of learning but don't know how. These are study skills. The term 'study skills' covers a variety of techniques that will make your studying activities easier and more effective. These techniques – all of which can be learned – include note taking, reading, writing essays and reports, planning, revising for examinations and sitting examinations.

Study skills also encompass the habits that you will need to acquire to become successful at studying. These habits establish patterns in your study timetable and ways of doing things that will help you to make the most of your study time. Of course, all these skills, habits and techniques have different components that will be useful at different times. Effective reading, for example, can be split into planning, skimming, speed reading, setting goals and developing a reading strategy and you will need all these components if you are to become proficient at reading to learn. Even if you already have one or more of these skills, you will be able to improve by following the advice and tips given in this book. In effect, you will learn how to learn. The major tasks that you will undertake as a student – writing essays, revising for and sitting exams, giving a presentation – all require a combination of study skills. To be successful, you will need to bring together the right techniques and habits and to have these skills at a sufficiently proficient level. While you are becoming proficient at the individual skills, you will also be developing the ability to combine the different skills as required.

Let's take the example of note taking. This is a very important study skill and one that you will find very difficult to manage without. In Chapter 4 on note taking you will find different ways of recording what you have learned from lectures or from your reading. Why not try them all? One will be sure to be more suitable for you than others and you will probably find that you will be able to use different methods in different situations. For instance, if you're brainstorming ideas prior to writing an essay, you may find it useful to use a spider diagram, jotting down ideas as they come into your head and then linking them up and organizing them into a suitable essay plan. If you're reading a difficult text and want to summarize it for future use or revision, you may want to use a highlighter pen to pick out the important bits in the text. If you currently have problems with note taking – perhaps you find it difficult to decide quite what you should be recording or you know only one method of taking notes – then reading this chapter will help you to develop your note taking skills so that you can take notes that are easy for you to understand, are well organized and, above all, relevant.

Of course, you will already have lots of skills that will be useful in your studies and, as I've already said, study skills are, like any other skill, made up of several elements. Some of these you may already have developed, even without knowing it. It might be that you are already a relatively fast reader or perhaps you are very organized and able to keep to deadlines. Such skills are obviously useful when studying. However, there are a whole host of other skills that you may have acquired throughout your life but which you might not so readily consider to be 'study skills'. These might include an ability to work independently, stamina, an analytical mind and an ability to concentrate. All these, too, will undoubtedly help you in your studies.

Check your skills

Knowing what skills you already have is very important, as this will enable you not only to make the most of these existing skills but also to identify where you need to improve. So now let's look at how you can identify the skills that will help you in studying. Sometimes it can be difficult to identify our own abilities and to see what we have to offer in any situation, so it can be a good idea to go through the exercise below with someone who knows you reasonably well and whom you can trust to be honest with you. Perhaps you can pair up with another student on your course for a discussion about this exercise so that you can, in turn, help them to discover their own skill sets.

Look at this list and, being as honest with yourself as possible, mark off all the skills you already possess, i.e. those where you feel you can give a reasonable performance:

▶ I am able to be succinct – *useful for both note taking and essays.* ☐
▶ I am organized – *vital for efficient studying.* ☐
▶ I am able to take instructions from others – *something you will inevitably have to do at several points during your course.* ☐

- ▶ I am good with numbers – *many courses contain some element of number work.* ☐
- ▶ I am self-disciplined – *always a useful skill when you have deadlines to meet.* ☐
- ▶ I am able to write letters and reports – *you may have learned this at work and it will help with the writing you will need to do to complete a course of study.* ☐
- ▶ I am computer literate – *a vital skill if you want to produce high-quality reports and essays or to use the Internet for research.* ☐
- ▶ I am able to learn from my mistakes – *some people tend to ignore their mistakes and problems and will therefore not find it easy to improve.* ☐
- ▶ I am determined to succeed – *determination to keep going will help you through the difficult times in your course.* ☐
- ▶ I am good at problem solving – *a valuable skill in many areas of your course, from the initial planning to working out how to pass your exams.* ☐
- ▶ I can read quickly – *if this is not a strong point for you, check out the chapter on effective reading skills.* ☐
- ▶ I have an ability to concentrate even under difficult circumstances – *this could enable you to study at odd moments in crowded places or when you have other problems on your mind.* ☐
- ▶ I am willing to ask for help when I need it – *everyone needs help sometimes, so don't be afraid to ask for it.* ☐
- ▶ I am a good negotiator – *this might help in group work or when you need to come to an agreement about deadline extensions.* ☐
- ▶ I am a team player – *an obvious advantage if you're working in groups.* ☐
- ▶ I am confident when speaking in public – *many courses require you to give an oral presentation.* ☐
- ▶ I am very creative – *this might help you with design elements of your course and the presentation of your assignments.* ☐
- ▶ I am not frightened of making decisions – *some people find themselves paralysed when a decision about their studies is*

needed, so the ability to make decisions can save time and torment. □

▶ I am good at putting my point across in a debate – *this will help not only in group work or online debates but also in putting essays together (an essay can be a bit like a debate with yourself).* □

▶ I find it easy to set priorities – *a vital skill when planning your study timetable.* □

▶ I can read and understand complex information – *an obvious help for a higher-level course.* □

▶ I can manage my stress levels – *stress can be debilitating and adversely affect your results so managing it is important.* □

▶ I can set goals for myself – *goals will help you get to where you want to be, so this is an essential skill.* □

▶ I am highly motivated – *this will lead to your meeting assignment deadlines and will enable you to keep going even when things get difficult.* □

▶ I manage my time well – *good time management at all stages of your course is essential.* □

▶ I can weigh up an argument easily – *arguments are the backbone of many academic texts and also of the assignments you will have to produce.* □

▶ I can organize information in a logical order – *this will be an indispensable skill when you are writing essays or reports or taking notes.* □

▶ I can find information from different sources – *this will help with research.* □

▶ I am good at seeing how things work – *this means that your level of understanding of many types of text or principles will be high.* □

▶ I work well under pressure – *with any course there will be times when pressure increases such as when assignments are due or at examination time.* □

▶ I can keep going until a task is finished – *having stamina can be important when you're studying as there may be times (for example, when you are facing an assignment deadline but you are late home from work or the children*

*are sick) when you will need to keep going even though
you are tired. You may need to work late into the night
on a complicated piece of work. For that you need staying
power and determination.* ☐

▶ I am able to work independently – *this is a vital attribute to
have when you are learning as a mature student as you will
not be 'force fed' all the necessary elements of your course
but will have to find things out for yourself.* ☐

▶ I have plenty of self-confidence – *having confidence in your
own abilities will help you to achieve just about anything.* ☐

▶ I am able to think analytically – *a useful skill when you're
reading academic texts or preparing essays and reports, for
which you will have to be able to weigh arguments for and
against a view put forward.* ☐

Were you surprised at just how many skills might be involved in
studying? And surprised, too, at how many of them you already
possess? These are all elements of the main skills you need to help
you in your studies and you will need to master many of them over
the course of your studies.

So, as you can see, study skills are vital and the ones that we do
not already possess can certainly be learned. If you follow the
advice in the appropriate chapters in this book and do the exercises
and the revision tests, you will certainly be able to improve your
study skills.

Study smarter – not harder or longer

Many people believe that, to be a successful student, it is necessary
to study into the night, making endless notes, reading until your
eyes hurt. This is not true. Of course, to pass exams and to get
good coursework scores requires plenty of work but it should
not be necessary to abandon all other things in your life or to do
so much studying that you feel exhausted. With the right skills,
applied in the right way, studying at any level can be easier than

that. Lots of things can help you to cut down on the amount of time that must be spent and on the effort that must be made to ensure good results. These include:

▶ *Making your notes brief and to the point – see Chapter 4.*
▶ *Reading more quickly – see Chapter 3.*
▶ *Being more selective in what you read – see Chapter 3.*
▶ *Planning ... and more planning – see Chapter 2.*
▶ *Managing your time – see Chapter 2.*

Working smarter – rather than harder or longer – is a vital skill for all students to learn, whatever their personal circumstances. You need to learn how to make every minute that you spend on your studies count. Your studying must be effective, so strategies like planning, time management, active learning and motivation are vital for success. So, don't just sit there staring at your books and notes and not making any progress – that is not effective study. Get organized, know your learning style, set your goals, engage with your notes and books and get great results – quicker.

Insight

If you find it difficult to settle down to study, limit your studying time to just 10 minutes. If, at the end of that time, you do not feel you've made progress, go and do something else. Plan your next study period into your schedule immediately.

Confidence is a very important element of working smarter. You need to know – and have complete belief – that you can succeed. In order to develop this level of self-belief, you need to learn the skills and to understand how all the components of these skills will ensure that you can do what you are setting out to do. You need to know, without any doubt, where you are going and how you are going to get there. Can you visualize yourself reaching the end of your course? Do you see yourself bathed in glory, completely satisfied with your performance and then going on to get that job you were aiming at, or all your family standing awestruck, finally convinced of your potential? Being able to visualize success is an important part of achieving it and is just one more study skill that you should practise often.

Of course, most people who start a new course of study worry about their abilities. They are afraid that they will fail. They are intimidated by all the unfamiliar things that they will be required to do – meeting new people in new places, reading academic texts, studying independently, writing assignments and sitting exams, to name but a few. But why are we all so afraid? Feelings of fear when facing something different are normal – almost everyone is scared when they first go to university or take their driving test, for example. It might appear, as you go on to the university campus for the first time or walk into the driving test centre, that everyone is calm, self-assured and comfortable in their surroundings. However, we can see that this is not the case if we examine our own reactions in this situation.

What do we do if we're almost paralysed with fear as we walk into a new situation? Do we turn to the person next in line to us, burst into tears, and say, 'I'm so frightened that I'm thinking of not doing this course. It's impossible. I just can't do it!'? No, of course we don't. We stand there appearing calm and self-assured – just like everyone else! We're all putting on an act. However, we must work hard to ensure that these feelings that we are hiding so well are not allowed to affect our chances of success. We might not let the outside world see how we feel but you can be sure that, inside, these insecure thoughts are having an effect. This is where the power of positive thinking comes into its own.

The power of positive thinking

There are plenty of self-help books on the market that will help you to develop a sense of self-belief and set you on the right path to building your self-confidence. The essence of positive thinking is that you can achieve more if your thoughts are positive ones rather than negative ones. When our internal voices are continually criticizing our performance, they are sabotaging our chances of success. When our minds are oriented in this way, we are set up to fail. If we can retrain ourselves to think positive thoughts and to believe that success is possible – no, that success is assured – then we will indeed be successful.

Insight

Prepare a few motivational statements for yourself – for example 'I am a hardworking, conscientious student' or 'I know I am going to succeed' – and repeat them to yourself at every opportunity.

There are several ways in which you can usefully engage in positive thinking during your time as a student and the first of these is to envisage positive outcomes. Do you see yourself passing your course? If not, then change your thinking right now. If you weren't capable of passing it, it is highly unlikely that you would be on the course at all. Set yourself some positive goals now. State them positively and in as much detail as you can muster. For example, you might say, 'I'm going to pass this course in the top 10 per cent of the class' or 'I am capable of meeting all my assignment deadlines this term.'

Visualization is a really important part of positive thinking and is often used by athletes. Do you think that they stand at the starting line, waiting for the gun to fire, with the thought that they will lose? That they see themselves coming last in the race? No, of course they don't. They use visualization repeatedly, seeing themselves breasting the tape, achieving their own personal best times, or doing the victor's lap of honour. The reasoning by all the top athletics coaches and sports psychologists is that positive thinking and visualization work and are vital elements in an athlete's training regime. The same is true for students. Picture yourself getting top results, emerging from the driving test centre waving your pass certificate, or getting that promotion at work and you will significantly enhance your chances of success. Play the scenes of your success like a DVD in your head – pushing the rewind button as often as you can – and you will come to believe it.

Your confidence will soar and, as if by magic, your results will improve.

A second way in which positive thinking can help you in your studies is by looking at your fears in a different way. This will help to diminish them. Let's go back to that queue where everyone is feeling afraid of what is to about to happen in their new situation. When you accept that everyone feels fear when they're attempting something new, you can see fear as something that is just part of being human. It is nothing to be ashamed of – it's just normal. Accept that and get on with your life. Of course, that doesn't make the fear go away. Can you think of anything that always makes fear go away? There is only one way. Fear will, without fail, disappear when we do whatever it is we're frightened of. We can feel terrified of leaping into the unknown, but, once we've made the leap and become accustomed to the new situation, we're no longer afraid. So, next time you're feeling frightened of something, don't try to live with the fear; instead face the fear and it will vanish.

Positive thinking can also help with the choices you make. Every time we're faced with a situation – a good experience or otherwise – we have a choice as to how we look at it and, in turn, this dictates how we deal with it. If you got a bad mark for an assignment, did you then think that it was the end of the world and it just proved you right in thinking that you hadn't got the hang of this subject? Or did you get the same mark and think 'So, what were the good bits in that essay? And what can I learn from what went wrong?' These two very different points of view will have different consequences. If you think it's a disaster, you're unlikely to make much improvement and might even be tempted to give up the course. If you can think positively and use all experiences – good or bad – to benefit you, you will be able to make improvements – in this case to your essay writing skills – and get a better mark next time.

Here are some tips to help you to think positively:

- ▶ Think of some positive statements about yourself – *I am hard working, I am a good student, I am good at this subject, I can write essays that get the message across. Be sure to state these in the positive, i.e. not 'I am not lazy, I am not a bad student, I'm not bad at this subject or I think I can write essays' and so on. Write these positive statements down and keep them where you can see them while you're studying.*

- ▶ Learn to assess your own work. *Do not allow yourself to think that passing or failing is a matter of luck or, worse, that you are doomed to failure because your work is simply not good enough. Discuss your marks with your tutors and understand what you have done wrong and, more importantly, what you have done right. Initiate discussions with other students about how they tackled assignments and then assess what you have done. Continuous improvement is possible by learning about your own work in this way and that will send your confidence soaring.*

- ▶ Meet up with some positive people. *We all know people who drag us down. They voice our fears – 'Do you really think you can cope with all that studying as well as your job?' or 'What are you studying for? It's a waste of time.' When you're feeling vulnerable, keep away from these people and seek out instead some people who will talk you up. They might say, 'Well done, you! Starting a new course takes courage' or 'Education is never lost – anyway it sounds really interesting.'*

- ▶ Mind your language. *Try to use positive words and think positive thoughts. This will cause a subtle change in how you feel and in the choices you make.*

- ▶ Accept responsibility for yourself and what happens to you. *Don't be a victim, forever thinking 'That always happens to me' or 'I'm just unlucky.' Instead, if something goes wrong, accept that it's happened and find out what you can do to make sure you do things better next time.*

Positive thinking has been proven to be beneficial in all areas of life and for all sorts of people – including students – so try out some of these ways of using positive thinking and increase your confidence.

Quick revision test

1 *Name three study skills that you will learn about in this book.*
2 *What are stated at the start of each chapter?*
3 *What is the essence of positive thinking?*
4 *What makes fear go away?*
5 *Why are the subjects in each chapter broken up into short sections?*

10 THINGS TO REMEMBER

1 You can use this book in two ways – either by reading right the way through it completing all of the exercises, tests and quizzes as you go along or by dipping into the chapters that cover the specific skills you need to improve on as and when you need to.

2 Do the quizzes at the end of each chapter – they will tell you if you have taken in the information you've read about in that chapter.

3 You need a wide range of skills to study effectively – many of which you already have; you should identify these first.

4 Study skills can be learned; with the help of this book you can master those skills you currently lack.

5 You should work smarter – not harder.

6 It is important to visualize success.

7 Conquer any fear you may have by using positive thinking; it is the main tool in gaining confidence in your abilities.

8 Use positive language when describing your reaction to your studying.

9 Prepare some positive statements about your abilities and use them to keep you motivated.

10 Learn to assess your own work by discussing it with your tutors and other students.

2

Getting organized

In this chapter you will learn:
- *how to manage your time*
- *how to make some space for studying*
- *how to get an overview of your course.*

Introduction

Getting organized is essential for successful study. Managing your time, getting your space set up properly and setting goals will bring dramatic improvements to your studies. Also, understanding what motivates you and managing your stress levels will help to make life easier and your studying more effective. So, let's look at the first thing you can do to get yourself organized.

Making a space for studying

Having your own space for studying and getting it organized will have many benefits. First, it will make your studying seem real. If you have been putting off starting some serious work on your course, you may find that having a desk set up with all your bits and pieces will finally motivate you into sitting down and getting on with it. Second, you will find it so much easier to pick up where you left off. If you don't have to waste time putting things away and then getting them out again when you next come to study, you will get so much more done and feel better about doing it. Other benefits include impressing on your family and friends that this business of studying is important to you; getting fewer interruptions because it will be obvious that you are studying if you are installed at your desk; and putting you in the right frame of mind for studying when you are at your workspace.

Having convinced ourselves of the usefulness and advantages of having an organized workspace, let's look first at some of the practical elements of getting organized. If you are continually having to clear a corner of the kitchen table for space to study or cannot find your calculator because last night you studied in a different place, then you will waste a huge amount of time getting ready to study rather than being able to plunge right into your work without wasting valuable time. Of course, life is not always perfect and it may be that you are simply unable to earmark a space that is solely for your use when studying. Maybe you have to share a space with other students or have to put everything away after each studying session so that the space can be used for something else. In this case, make sure that you are able to store your books, notes and equipment safely. Clear out a nearby drawer for this purpose, or, at a pinch, you could buy a large plastic storage box and use that. Ideally, though, you need to get your hands on your own exclusive space, so let's look at this in a bit more detail.

Your first priority must be to decide on your space for studying. Where will it be? Ideally, it will be a space of your own where you will be able to get organized and then leave your things ready for you to come back to them after each break in your studying. In considering the space you have, your minimum requirements should include:

▶ *a writing surface with plenty of space for your books, papers, pens, etc.*
▶ *at least one bookshelf*

- *room for your computer if you have one*
- *a light in the correct place – not shining on to your computer screen or into your eyes – and which is suitable for reading by*
- *a chair at the correct height for your computer and for your desk for writing (remember that you will be spending some time in this chair so it should be comfortable and support your back).*

Your setup will, to a certain extent, depend on whether or not you have a computer. Most people do these days but it may be that you have decided that you can manage with the facilities provided at college, university, at work or in libraries.

Insight

Keep your working space tidy and well organized. If it always looks a mess then you will be far less likely to want to come back to it.

Having created an efficient space for your study area, you will now need to organize it so that everything is to hand. Make sure that you have plenty of files so that your notes and handouts can be filed away in a way that makes it easy to find them when you need them. Simply piling everything up and hoping that you will be able to lay your hands on them at some future date will not save you time in the long run. You will lose vital pieces of information and waste precious time and patience shuffling through papers over and over again.

Other things that you will find useful – or even essential – to keep in this area will include:

- *course books – some you will have had to buy and others you will be able to borrow from a library*
- *a diary or wall planner so that you can note the dates on which assignments are due*
- *plenty of A4 paper – plain copier paper if you are using a computer and lined, punched paper for handwritten notes*

- ▶ *ring files – it's a good idea to use a different-coloured ring file for each different subject that you're studying*
- ▶ *a dictionary and a thesaurus*
- ▶ *a calculator*
- ▶ *assorted items of equipment such as a stapler, a hole punch, glue and sticky tape, correcting fluid, ruler, highlighters, pens and pencils, small notepads, spare disks for your computer, scissors and so on.*

You should find a space for all these things when you are setting up your study area. Don't just put them on the workspace, thinking you'll get organized later – do it now and save yourself lots of time and frustration. Keep the space tidy by filing loose notes as soon as you've made them (use A4 paper rather than reporter's pads or notebooks to make this easier) and putting everything away when you've finished for the day.

If you have a computer as part of your studying setup, you will need to organize that too. The first – and most important – piece of advice about working with a computer is to *back up your files*. Keep backup copies of everything that you've saved to the hard drive and also of anything you have on floppy, ZIP or CD disk. Don't be tempted to leave this job – it's vital. Just imagine how you would feel if your computer crashed and you lost that essay you'd just spent days researching, organizing and writing. Work out how many hours it would take you to rewrite that piece of work (and add on the time you would spend desperately searching your hard drive in an attempt to get it back). It would take a lot longer than getting organized would, right? Then back up your files! Apart from making sure that you have backup copies of all your work, there are other things you can do to ensure that you keep your computer and all the hard work you do with it in tip-top order:

- ▶ *Use a separate disk for saving each subject.*
- ▶ *Keep your disks safe in a storage box, with all the disks suitably labelled.*

> **Insight**
> An alternative to using separate disks for storage is to invest
> in an external hard drive. They can be connected to your
> computer but keep a copy of all your files separately. It's a
> good idea to back up your files on a regular basis, so make it
> part of your routine.

▸ *Use a different folder on your hard drive for each subject
  that you are studying. Within these folders you can then use
  sub-folders for assignments, notes, etc. There is more advice
  about using your computer to learn in Chapter 9.*

▸ *Name files on the hard drive so that you immediately know
  what is in that file. Don't be tempted to use dates and very
  abbreviated titles – you'll forget what is in the file and waste
  time opening them to check them out when you're looking
  for a particular file.*

▸ *Whether it's your computer or your desk and your notes,
  the most important thing to remember is that getting it
  organized – and keeping it that way – will save you time.*

> **Insight**
> Don't let 'getting organized' become a way of avoiding
> getting down to the actual studying.

Making time for studying

In addition to finding and organizing the physical space for
studying, you must also consider how you will find and organize
the time in your schedule. We all have the same 24 hours in a
day – that's 168 hours every week – but some people seem to find
the time to do far more than others. The reality is that we have
choices as to how we spend our time in just the same way as we
all have choices about how we spend our money. Some habits and
personality traits become a drain on our time resources and it is
these that we need to change if we want to spend our time wisely.
We can all achieve more if we learn a bit about time management

and then put what we have learned into action. Use this checklist to see if you have too many drains on your time resources.

Tick each box that applies to you:

1 *I am easily distracted.* ☐
2 *I am often late for appointments.* ☐
3 *I have not set myself achievable goals.* ☐
4 *I do not understand what motivates me.* ☐
5 *I check my e-mails more than twice a day.* ☐
6 *I frequently put things off.* ☐
7 *I chat for hours on the phone – even when I have a deadline to meet.* ☐
8 *I frequently stop when I am working to make a cup of tea or coffee.* ☐
9 *I read absolutely everything I am told to read.* ☐
10 *I don't keep a diary.* ☐

Give yourself one mark for each answer you have ticked and add up your score and check it as follows:

If you scored 1 or 2

You don't have much of a problem with time management when you are studying. Read the remainder of this section to pick up a few tips to help you and then simply keep going.

If you scored 3 to 5

You have a few issues with time management and will benefit from putting some of the advice that follows in this section into practice.

If you scored 6 to 8

Your lack of time management skills will be causing problems, so read the remainder of this section carefully and, most importantly, take action. Do not put it off.

(Contd)

If you scored 9 or 10

You need some help to manage your time. You are probably not managing your time at all and will be wasting a lot of it. Read the advice that follows, then make some changes to your routines.

Insight

Having done the questionnaire, don't just ignore what it tells you about your approach to time management. Take some action.

Before we look at time management in a bit more detail, here are the basics of improving how you manage your time:

- ▶ *Do not procrastinate.*
- ▶ *Set achievable goals.*
- ▶ *Keep track of your time.*
- ▶ *Stay focused.*
- ▶ *Get organized.*
- ▶ *Plan to succeed.*

Although we all have the same number of hours to spend, many of us have extra demands on our time and it can be incredibly difficult to juggle all these demands. It may be that you have a small child – or several – who need care on a daily basis, older children who have hectic social lives and you are their taxi service, a challenging teenager to deal with or an elderly relative to care for. Or you may have a stressful job with long hours that leaves you feeling drained when you return home. However, whatever your commitments, you have decided to pursue a course of study so you need to learn to juggle your commitments so that you spend your time to the best possible effect. Having chosen to study, you must give that your best shot or it will have been a waste of time to start the course. So, what can you do to decide how to allocate your time effectively and to lessen your responsibilities so that you have more time available for your studies?

Time-saving tips

Find out how you spend your time now. Unless you know *exactly* what you are doing with the 24 hours you have available to you every day, then you will not be able to make any effective changes. Write down everything you do from getting up to going to bed – cleaning your teeth, feeding the dog, travelling, sitting doing nothing – absolutely everything. This is known as a *time audit.* If you can do this for a whole week, you will find that this is a very enlightening exercise. Then add up how much time you spend on regular tasks and pastimes such as sleeping, travelling, working, eating and so on.

Subtract all these chunks of time from the 168 hours in a week and see what you're left with. Invariably there will be a leftover period and this is how much time you already have available – without making a single change to your daily life and habits – to spend on your new task of studying. Now look at exactly what you are doing during a week and how much time you're spending on non-essential things. Do you need to spend half an hour every day reading a newspaper? Could you group all your phone calls together on one evening and limit the time you spend on each? Could you go food shopping once a week instead of two or three times? Revising your habits in any of these areas could yield a couple of hours every single week – enough time to write a report or plan out an essay.

Insight

In these busy times, everyone feels overworked and as if they haven't got time for any more tasks – but we all waste some time during a week and it is this wasted time that we need to find and use to better effect.

MAKE A PLAN

Get a large day-to-a-page diary or make yourself a 24-hour planner on your PC and put all your commitments in it – include work, exercise, sleep, your family duties and a little 'slack' where you'll be able to catch up on things that have slipped a little or take longer than you thought ... and don't forget to add your social life! Now you should be able to see just where you will be able to allocate time to your studies. Look carefully for those times when you have not planned anything specific to do. Look also for the things that you are planning in but which are not essential or errands that could be grouped together to save you time. Could you get up an hour earlier or go to bed later to enable you to fit in everything you want – or need – to do?

Then write in all your assignment deadlines and exam dates and plan in all the extra time you will need to spend on your studying at these times. Now, write in your studying schedule where you can fit it in. Actually writing it down – as you would a dental appointment or family visit – will make it seem more like a commitment. If you can make this plan visible to your partner and children or others who feel they have a call on your time – then you will have an even greater chance of making your plan work. Alternatives to using a diary or your PC to record your activities and to plan your time could include A4 paper in a loose-leaf file, an electronic organizer or a specially designed time management planner. You must choose the method that works best for you.

Plan both long term and short term

You could start with a general academic year planner where you will get an overview of what's ahead of you, then move on to planning for the term to come and work your way through to a monthly plan and then go into real detail on a weekly study planner.

CREATE NEW HABITS

Use your diary to record each time you succeed in following your new habits. At first, all changes in behaviour require thought but if you do it for three or four weeks consecutively (and make an effort to record it, which reinforces the habit) you will soon find that you can do it automatically.

SET SOME RULES

If everyone who is affected by the time you will have to spend
on your course knows what is expected of them, it will be a lot
easier to keep to your plans and to meet your goals. Rules you
might like to consider could include 'Nobody to interrupt me
while I'm studying unless it is really urgent.' You may have to
review this rule and give some guidelines as to what you consider
to be urgent if you find that you are interrupted for demands
for snacks or help in finding lost possessions. What you decide
regarding what is urgent is what everyone will have to abide by.
Another rule that might help is that 'Everyone picks up and puts
away their own belongings.' Even very small children are capable
of doing this, so don't hesitate. You have different priorities now
and waiting on everyone will not fit in with your studying.
Make rules, too, that you will have to follow – such as no studying
after midnight (unless you're a night owl) or no studying on
Sunday afternoons if this is usually a time that you spend with
the family.

STEAL A FEW MINUTES

Grab small chunks of time whenever you can. A lot can be
achieved in small time slots. If you have a 20-minute bus journey
every morning, then make sure that you use this time to move
your studying efforts forward. Plan an essay, read an article or a
chapter of a set book or make a few notes about something you
read the previous day. If you drive to work or back from the school
run, record tapes of revision notes so that you can listen to them
as you drive. You may find that you are unable to concentrate
for the whole of the tape but that, if you play it often enough, you
will absorb plenty of information and will have avoided wasting
your time in a traffic jam. You could also read in the bath or in
your lunch hour at work. You will soon find that if you can
snatch a few minutes in this way every day you will have achieved
a lot without too much disruption to your life by the end of
the week.

DELEGATE

It is almost always true to say that you are not the only person who can deal with the tasks you have taken on. Do you drive your son or daughter to various activities every evening? Could you share this task with another child's parents? Take turns at this task (or delegate it to your partner, perhaps) and you will have several hours extra to enable you to get stuck into an assignment for your course.

THE 80:20 RULE

This rule says that 20 per cent of your time will be spent on productive work while the remaining 80 per cent will be spent on tasks that are lower priority, unproductive or unnecessary. You must find your 80 per cent and cut out as much of the work in that 80 per cent as you possibly can. If you are fanatical about keeping your house clean, for example, decide how often you really need to dust or vacuum – could you miss this job out occasionally and allocate the time you've saved to studying? Do you watch television programmes that you haven't specifically chosen to watch – you just sit there after your favourite programme has ended and continue to watch until it's time for bed? Cut out those programmes and you'll be surprised at how much time you have freed up. Do you have a lie-in on weekend mornings? Could you have a lie-in on either Saturday or Sunday rather than both? Or could you set a slightly earlier time to get up than at present but still treating yourself to a little extra time in bed?

GET ORGANIZED

If everyone in the family could write their social commitments down on a wall planner, it will save time that you currently spend asking everyone what they're doing at the weekend or it may stop your daughter surprising you with a request to collect her from a friend's house just when you'd started a complicated piece of work for your course. Another way that getting organized will save you time is that you will not waste time looking for things on a regular basis if your cupboards and drawers are tidy and everything put back in place after use.

TALK TO YOUR FAMILY

Explain to them what you are trying to achieve and how important your studying is to you. It is essential that you enlist their support if you are to achieve your aims. If you have previously spent all your spare time catering to their needs, it may be difficult at first for them to accept that you will sometimes have to put their requirements second and that you will be spending time doing something for you, but if you can make them understand the situation and ask for their help in achieving your goals, most family members will be cooperative. Ask them how they think they can help you – you may be surprised at some of the ideas they come up with and with the level of support they are prepared to give you.

Insight

Do ask for help – most people close to you will be prepared to help you if you make it clear that something is important to you.

INTRODUCE CHANGES GRADUALLY

Do not make the changes all at once, as this will be far too painful both for you and your family. If you need help to run the house then have a week where your family helps with one small job. When you've got that up and running, introduce another change at home. This also applies at work. If your aim is to leave on time every evening instead of working late, you may need to leave on time on one day per week for a while and then start cutting down on the time you work on other days until you have reduced your hours to a more manageable level.

MAKE GOOD USE OF LISTS

Each week, make a list of all the things you plan to achieve that week – research goals, progress towards an assignment and so on – and then cross off each item as and when you have completed it. Not only is this an organized approach that will prevent you from forgetting some vital task but it can also be very satisfying to cross things off the list. It will give you a sense of achievement and keep you motivated.

REVIEW YOUR PROGRESS REGULARLY

Keep track of how closely you've stuck to your plans and how much progress you've made towards your goals. If you're going off track you need to find this out as soon as possible and then take corrective action. There is little point in making elaborate plans with every assignment noted down, revision time planned in and time blocked out for lectures if you ignore the plan and make little or no progress and then realize this only when you fail your exams at the end of your course. You need to know about problems and rectify them or get help.

DON'T PUT IT OFF

We are all guilty of some level of procrastination but if we want to achieve anything in our lives, we must get on and do it. This rule of 'do it now' applies to the things we must do to manage our time as well as to the tasks we must do to complete a course of study. It helps if you understand why you are putting something off and the most common reason associated with starting an essay or other assignment is the fear of failure. Conquer your fear of failure (if you don't start, you'll never, ever finish) and make a start.

Insight

In your efforts to save time, do not be tempted to eliminate completely the activities that relax you. Keeping yourself fit, healthy and relaxed is essential to allow you to work to your full potential.

If you're still looking for just a bit more time to save, take a look at your study methods and see where you could work more efficiently:

- Never rewrite. *Your notes don't need to be super-neat, so don't waste time writing them out again. Write assignments directly on to your computer rather than writing them first in longhand (remember you can use the cut and paste facility later if you need to change the order around slightly).*
- Focus. *Don't work on things that will not take you closer to your goals or spend too much time on relatively simple, short assignments.*
- Be brief. *Your notes should not be a word-for-word repetition of what the lecturer has said or a rambling essay on a book or article you've read. They should be short, so use lots of headings and write in key words and phrases rather than complete sentences.*
- Be tidy. *If you know where all your notes are and they're filed away in a logical order, you won't waste time searching for one piece of information or for the notes you know will help you to complete an assignment. File your notes away as soon as you've made them so that the filing task doesn't get out of hand.*
- Make filing easy. *Use a separate piece of paper for every topic so that you can file them in a logical order and then file them in a lever arch file so that you can extract them as needed.*

Understanding your learning style

The way we learn differs from person to person and many ways of classifying learning styles have been tried. One of the most popular analyses of ways we learn centres on the senses we use to absorb information – the *primary learning pathway*. It is helpful to find our own learning style as this will ensure that we can look out for ways to learn that are appropriate for us and will make learning easier. The three learning styles that have been defined by psychologists working on neuro-linguistic programming (NLP) projects are:

- visual – *this is where learning is sight based*
- auditory – *here the primary sense involved in learning is hearing*
- kinaesthetic – *this involves the sense of touch.*

Try this quick quiz to discover your learning style. A lot of the clues to defining our learning style can be found in the things we say or how we tackle everyday tasks. Read these questions and decide which answer you would be more likely to give:

1 **When checking the spelling of a word what to do you say?**
   a   That looks right.
   b   That sounds right.
   c   That feels right.

2 **If you're trying to reassure someone that you understand what they are saying to you, what do you say?**
   a   I can see what you're saying.
   b   I hear what you're saying.
   c   I feel that I understand what you're saying.

3 **If you're buying a new piece of furniture or equipment for your home, what would influence your decision the most?**
   a   How it looks.
   b   The description given by the salesperson.
   c   How it feels when you touch it.

4 **What would be most useful to you if you were trying to assemble this new item of furniture or equipment?**
   a   A video of it being assembled.
   b   Recorded instructions.
   c   Trying to do it yourself.

5 **What would help you to understand a mathematical problem?**
   a   Diagrams about how it can be solved.
   b   Listening to someone's explanation of the solution.
   c   A model of how it all fits together.

6 **If you're trying to understand some new computer software, what would you do?**
   a   Read the manual that came with the software.
   b   Ask a friend to come over and tell you how they use it.
   c   Sit at the keyboard trying it out.

7 **If you are looking for something to buy in a bookshop, what makes you choose a particular book?**

   a   The look of the cover.

   b   A friend talking about it and saying it was worth reading.

   c   The book feels heavy and glossy.

8 **How are you most likely to give someone directions to your home?**

   a   Writing the directions down.

   b   Telling them which roads to take.

   c   Drawing them a map.

9 **Think back to when you were at school. Which sort of lessons did you most enjoy?**

   a   Where the teachers drew diagrams or gave us a textbook.

   b   Where the teacher told us about a subject.

   c   Practical sessions.

10 **Where would you be most likely to find a review of a film that makes you want to go to see it?**

   a   In a newspaper or magazine.

   b   On the radio or from a friend telling you about it.

   c   On the TV.

Now add up all your *a*'s, *b*'s and *c*'s and check out the styles below.

If you got mostly a's

Your learning style is visual. You learn best by seeing things. This might be by reading books or by watching television or educational videos. Anything you can do to enhance the visual impact of your learning materials will improve your learning experience and help you to remember what you have learned. For you, it will be a good idea to use different coloured highlighters and pencils when making your notes and to make sure that you include plenty of spider diagrams (more about these in Chapter 4), tables and graphs in your revision materials.

(Contd)

You will know that you are a visual person if you say things like 'I see what you mean' or 'I can't see what the problem is.'

If you got mostly b's

Your learning style is auditory and the most important sense that you use in learning is that of hearing. You will learn best by discussing things with fellow students or listening to audio tapes or lectures. Debates will help you tremendously and, if you find something difficult to understand, you could try explaining it to someone else who has no knowledge of the subject. Your revision can be helped along by recording yourself reading your notes out loud (keep them brief or you'll spend too long doing the recording) and then playing the tapes back to yourself repeatedly.

The things that you will say that will show that hearing is your primary learning pathway include 'Sounds OK to me' and 'I hear what you're saying.'

If you got mostly c's

Your learning style is kinaesthetic. This means that the sense of touch is most important to you. Practical learning sessions will help you to retain information so you should make sure that you take part in as many experiments as you can and get hold of practical objects in connection with your studies that you are able to feel and touch.

The clues in the language you use that show that touch is most important to you include 'It feels good to me' or 'That touched a nerve!'

Although everyone will have a dominant sense that dictates their learning style, the very best approach for all students is one that uses a combination of all three senses to get the message across. Individual students will need to be aware of their own preferences and then play to their strengths as we have just detailed, while using materials that combine all the learning styles. Now that you know what is likely to work best for you, seek out the type of materials that suit you and will help you to retain the information you will need to be successful in your studies.

Do not, however, let knowing your learning style blind you to all the other ways to learn. If you concentrate exclusively on methods that you think will suit your way of learning you may miss something that would really help you. It is important, while knowing and catering for your learning style, to experiment with different methods of learning. We are all a mixture of styles and personality traits and these can change according to our mood and what's going on in our lives, so we must remain open-minded about learning methods.

Motivation

The single most important factor in whether or not you will find a course enjoyable and productive is motivation. If you are highly motivated and genuinely want to make a success of your studies, then chances are you will. If you really want to improve your study skills, then reading this book and putting its principles into practice will ensure that you arm yourself with a set of skills that you can use in whatever course of study you choose to undertake. Of course, you must do more than acquire study skills – you must be prepared to put in the work that will make the most of these skills and ensure that you can complete your course of study successfully.

Some people seem to be motivated to do things and it is difficult to see how they have achieved this motivated state. Partly this is probably because of their personalities – these fortunate people are usually optimists who have high levels of self-belief and determination to achieve. Typically, they will see any problems that may crop up as challenges to be overcome or as opportunities to show what they can do. But if you are a little unsure of yourself and can see only difficulties when you contemplate your new course of study, then you need to build your self-confidence (take a look back at Chapter 1 for some more tips on confidence) and work on your motivation.

Motivation is often all about our reasons for wanting to achieve something, so examining why you want to take – and pass! – your course will help with focusing on and increasing your motivation. If you can identify positive outcomes that really matter to you, and keep working towards these rather than just forcing yourself into the drudgery of studying, you will be on the way to becoming more motivated. Complete this quick quiz to help you identify your motivating factors.

Here is a list of possible reasons you may have for taking your course. Pick the five most important reasons for you:

- ▶ *to get a specific job* ☐
- ▶ *to use it as a stepping stone to further qualifications* ☐
- ▶ *to gain promotion at work* ☐
- ▶ *to earn more money* ☐
- ▶ *to learn about a subject that I find interesting* ☐
- ▶ *to change my life* ☐
- ▶ *to improve my prospects* ☐
- ▶ *to gain control of my life* ☐
- ▶ *to prove to myself that I can achieve something* ☐
- ▶ *to prove to my family and/or friends that I am intelligent* ☐
- ▶ *because all my friends are going on to further education* ☐
- ▶ *to get a better social life* ☐
- ▶ *to make up for wasting my educational opportunities when I was younger.* ☐

Now put your five reasons in order of importance and think about them carefully. Knowing just why you're doing something is usually enough to supply motivation – especially if the reasons are compelling enough and you can see how the course will serve you.

Insight

Keep this list of your motivational factors somewhere where you can see it. Make sure that you look at it frequently during your studies, as it will help to get you through the inevitable rough patches.

One thing getting in the way of your motivation may be stress. We'll look at how we can keep this under control in the next section.

Managing stress

There are many different stresses involved in studying. You may be a student away from home and finding it difficult to study independently for the first time or you may be a mature student with myriad demands from your family or your employers on your mind. You may feel that the course of study you have taken on is beyond your capabilities or you may be feeling that you have nowhere to turn to for help with the work you have to do. Some of the causes of stress may not be related to your study. You may have money worries or one of your close family members may be ill. Whatever the cause of your stress, the important thing is not to let it overwhelm you.

A low level of stress can have a positive effect on your ability to study. If you were not bothered in the slightest by a looming deadline for an assignment, it is highly unlikely that you would produce the best work that you could, and on time. If, by the same token, the assignment is on your mind for several days before it is due and you worry about meeting the deadline, then you are more likely to deliver a competent piece of work on schedule. What is not desirable is an excessively high level of stress. If you are really

affected by the amount or difficulty of work you have to produce
or the deadlines that you must adhere to, then you may start to
display some symptoms such as:

▶ *becoming irritable and easily upset*
▶ *having difficulty sleeping*
▶ *eating, smoking or drinking too much in an effort to calm*
  your nerves
▶ *spending too much time (i.e. all of your spare time) studying*
▶ *thinking that everyone is doing better than you*
▶ *becoming clumsy*
▶ *feeling sick at the thought of an assignment.*

If you feel like this, you must get help. These are all symptoms of
stress and it must be managed so that it is not allowed to affect
your health. Wherever and however you are studying there will be
sources of support available; you must search them out. If you are
at university there will be a whole range of support services. Your
first port of call should usually be your tutor. He or she will be able
to deal with specific difficulties you may be having with any of the
course material and may also have experience in dealing with more
general stress.

Your student union will usually have officers able to offer support
and, of course, all these services will be confidential. If you are
studying a work-related course, then the course tutors or your
boss/personnel department may all be able to offer support. If
you are doing a distance-learning course, you will still have a
tutor who will be responsible for offering you help to complete
the course successfully. Whichever route you take, the important
thing is to get help before it becomes a serious issue. If you allow
the problem to get gradually worse and perhaps move from being
something that causes you the occasional twinge of discomfort to
something that is in danger of seriously damaging your mental and
physical health, your coursework may suffer and you will find it
increasingly difficult to get yourself back on track. If the situation
has become serious, apart from seeking help from your tutor or
others involved in your studying, you may need to approach your

doctor for help with coping with the symptoms of depression or stress.

It is well known that severe stress can affect memory and brain function as energy is diverted to deal with the stress. If you think that you are suffering from relatively mild stress and want to take steps at a very early stage to help yourself, then you should:

▶ Make sure you get enough sleep – *an hour spent having a nap (occasionally!) will be beneficial and you must try to get a regular six to seven hours' sleep at night, as this is when the brain will refresh itself.*
▶ Plan in some activities that you find relaxing – *reading a book for pleasure or listening to music will pay dividends in terms of making you more relaxed and refreshed ready for your studying task.*
▶ Getting organized will make you feel less stressed – *put some of the ideas earlier in this chapter into practice.*
▶ Get to know yourself – *consider what causes you to feel stressed. Keeping a note of times when you feel most stressed will highlight these occasions and then you can make plans to deal with them. It helps to jot down your feelings about these stressful times and situations and then to note your options for resolving the situation. You can then decide, in a calm, unstressed way, how to deal with things that bother you. Taking an organized approach to your stress like this will mean that you can make steady progress through your course without letting stress build up.*
▶ Deal with the most important things first. *If you have a number of things on your mind that are beginning to bother you, you could list them, prioritize them according to urgency and importance, and then deal with them one by one. You will find that dealing with just one thing at a time – and knowing that this is the highest priority – will immediately take the stress out of most situations.*
▶ Realize that you are not the only one. *Most of your fellow students will be feeling anxious about all sorts of things – including the very same things that are worrying you. They*

will be wondering what everyone else thinks of them, whether everyone else is finding the course easier than they are, whether they will be able to cope with the workload, whether they will meet their next assignment deadline and so on. Many students, especially mature students with family responsibilities, will also be worrying about their finances, childcare facilities, family reactions to their studies, finding the confidence to make friends, job commitments and so on. The solution to this is to get together, if at all possible, with other students. Form a support group, a study group, a social group or an online group – any one of these will help you to realize that your worries are common ones and you will benefit from others' experience.

▶ Get some exercise – *getting outdoors for a while or doing something that uses up energy (it could be going to the gym, jogging or walking, gardening, swimming or even a bit of housework) will make you feel better and more relaxed. Getting plenty of exercise will also ensure that you sleep well to boost memory.*

▶ Try meditation – *if you can learn how to do this you may be able to think more clearly and see your way through your temporary difficulties. A simple way to start is to sit quietly and simply focus on your breathing. Breathe in, breathe out and keep doing this until your mind is quiet. If thoughts intrude, acknowledge them and let them go, then go back to concentrating on your breathing. If you persevere, you will find that you become relaxed. There are many books about meditation that you could try if this is the sort of thing that you feel would help you.*

▶ Eat well – *aim to keep your blood sugar level in good balance to ensure efficient brain functioning. Eat a wide variety of foods including plenty of fruit, vegetables and whole grains.*

▶ Drink plenty of water – *if you wait until you're thirsty before you drink, then you are probably already dehydrated. Dehydration can affect your ability to remember and to concentrate. Don't be tempted to drink too much coffee instead of water – caffeine can give you an initial boost but will soon cause a lack of concentration.*

Stress can be helpful if it gives you the impetus to get up and get going. If it gets beyond that, then you should take action. If it's mild then you can help yourself, but if it is severe than you need to tap into the support that will be there for you in various forms. If it becomes more acute it will rapidly affect your coursework and will usually result in your missing deadlines and suffering a lack of concentration – neither of which will enhance your chances of getting a good result from your studies. Make sure that stress does not affect your results. Severe stress is not inevitable; it can be managed so that you keep your stress levels under control.

Insight

Managing stress is often about maintaining a balance in your life. It is not a good idea to do one thing to the exclusion of everything else.

Getting an overview of your course

Often when you first start a new course of study, your enthusiasm is high and you just want to dive right in. You rush out and buy the set books, perhaps mark your assignments on your shiny, new wall planner and enter the exam dates in your diary. But you shouldn't. Your first task should be to get an overview of your course. This will put you in the driving seat as it will help you to prepare for what is to come. If you take control at this very early stage, you will find that your motivation and energy for the course will soar. You will be able to see clearly where you are going and what your goals are.

How can you take control in this way? If you're lucky, there will be an easy way to get an overview of your course. Often your course tutors or designers will have prepared a summary of the course that details the required learning outcomes. It may also have a paragraph or two that give the aims of the course. Don't be tempted to ignore these paragraphs, as they are very important. Knowing what you are aiming for is vital. As soon as you're accepted on to a course you should find out if a booklet of this kind has been produced and, if so, get hold of a copy without delay. This will be your map for your studies. It tells you where you are going. You will then be able to work out how you are going to get there.

Your next step in gaining an overview should be to find out exactly how the course is going to be assessed. It may be that the only thing that matters in whether you are judged to have passed or failed the course is the mark you get in the examination at the end of the course. Alternatively, your coursework may also be taken into account or even the entire course mark may be based on the marks you get for your assignments. When you know how the assessment works, you will be able to see where the bulk of your time should be spent. If the course is based on continuous assessment, then you will have to make sure that every single piece of work that you complete – be it an essay, a report, a computer-marked assignment or a presentation – should be as good as you can make it. In this case there will be no room for coasting along during the year and then revising furiously for the end-of-year exam. Having said that, coasting is not a good idea even if the course result depends solely on the exam. In this case, steady progress, understanding all the different aspects of your course and sorting out problems as you go along will get you the best results and be far less stressful. However, if the course result does depend on how you do in the final examination, then you will obviously need to plan in time for the extra revision involved.

There are various other sources of information that will help you to get an overview of your course and give you plenty of clues as to how you should be tackling your studies. These include past examination papers, timetables and assignment details. It is important that you combine all these additional sources of information about your course with what you have found out about the expected learning outcomes and assessment. Go through all the materials you have collected and highlight or make a separate note of how each session, assignment or exam question ties in with each of the learning outcomes. It can be a good idea to write each of the learning outcomes on a separate sheet of paper, then seek out and add to each sheet all the things (e.g. assignments or exam questions) that contribute to that particular learning outcome. Having done this it will become clear just how you are going to get from where you are now to where you want to be at the end of the course. Do not rush this task. You will find it useful and productive to allow yourself plenty of time to reflect on the journey you are about to take. If you can think clearly now and get straight in your mind the way in which you are going to tackle your studies, it will pay dividends later.

Insight

Knowing what is expected of you is essential. An overview of your course will answer a lot of your questions in the early days of your course.

Gaining an overview of a course is an important part of becoming an effective learner and is therefore an essential study skill to master. You should do this before you start any other work on your course so that you can see what you are aiming at and how you are going to get there. Your goals will become clearer and you will have developed a map through your studies for yourself.

Quick revision test

1 *Name three of the things you need to arrange – as a minimum – for your study space.*
2 *What is the most important thing to do on a regular basis when using a computer for study?*
3 *Give two ways that you can save time while studying.*
4 *Name the three different learning styles discussed in this chapter.*
5 *Give two symptoms of severe stress.*

10 THINGS TO REMEMBER

1   *Get organized – find your own space where you can study to improve your productivity, reduce interruptions and help you achieve a better frame of mind.*

2   *Always back up computer files and do so frequently.*

3   *Find your wasted time – everyone wastes some time so find yours and use it for studying.*

4   *Set achievable goals – having a plan will help you to succeed.*

5   *Use a diary to help you plan your time effectively and check your progress regularly.*

6   *Get some support – from your family, friends, tutors and other students.*

7   *Try to understand your learning style – visual (where learning is sight based), auditory (where the primary sense involved in learning is hearing) or kinaesthetic (involving the sense of touch) – and then play to your strengths.*

8   *Decide what will motivate you to study such as writing down five of the most important reasons you have for doing your course and use it to keep you going.*

9   *If you think that you have anything other than a low level of stress – which can be beneficial – take steps to reduce it.*

10 *Get an overview of your course as soon as you start. It will help you to see what you are aiming for so you can plan how you will get there. You will know that you are a visual person if you say things like 'I see what you mean' or 'I can't see what the problem is.'*

3

Effective reading

Introduction

Reading is central to any studying task so it is vital that you do it as effectively and efficiently as you possibly can. Now, if you're saying 'But I can read already!', you must take into account that being able to make sense of words on a page is not the same as learning from your reading. There are a number of reading strategies that you can adopt to ensure that what you read is useful and appropriate to your course of study and also that you read in an organized way and retain a lot of what you read so that you can use it in the future.

If you have problems with reading – perhaps because of dyslexia or some other difficulty – get help early. Your tutors will have ways to make things easier or will be able to point you in the direction of some practical help and support.

How reading for study is different from reading for pleasure

Learning is an active pursuit. It is not something that just happens. When we read to learn, we need to actively gather information, make sense of it and organize it so that we can use it effectively to get the best return from the time we invest in our study. And, of course, in most cases we need to memorize certain aspects of what we have read so that we can use the information to help us pass exams. Reading for pleasure, by the same token, is something that we can do while we're relaxing; we can let a favourite book or the morning's newspaper just wash over us and we don't necessarily remember any of it. Mostly we make no effort at all to remember it; we just take the pleasure from it. When reading for pleasure we may choose newspapers, magazines, romantic, historical, mystery or thriller novels and non-fiction books featuring subjects of particular interest to us. We read things that appeal to us for a variety of reasons and then we let them go.

In contrast to this, reading for study means that we have to read totally different materials and make a concerted effort to remember them. We may be faced by a seemingly endless reading list of books, journals and Internet research materials – and we may not have chosen to read any of these things had we not been doing this particular course of study.

Studying will be infinitely easier if we can engage with our subject and have a genuine interest in at least part of it. When we take part in academic reading we are aiming to increase our knowledge of the subject and we also have the aim of passing our course of study. At first, this will seem like an impossible task but it does become easier as we become more familiar with what is required of us. Academic reading is done in stages. First, we read to gain a general understanding of our subject and some background knowledge. As we learn more and add to this background knowledge, we move on to developing the ideas that are new to us and then to finding different opinions and arguments about different areas of our subject.

Insight

It is important to focus on what you are reading and to make connections as you read – with past knowledge and with other parts of your course.

As academic reading is different from reading simply for pleasure, we must approach the task in a different way. We need to have a strategy, to set goals for our reading and to have ways of knowing whether we have achieved what we set out to do. For this we need to plan and this is the topic covered in the next section.

Planning your reading task and setting goals

If you are reading to study, you will need to have a reading strategy to ensure that you get the most from your hard work. Do not just pick up a book from the recommended reading list for your course, start reading at page one and then plough painfully through the book until you get to the end. This will be time-consuming, boring and not very effective. Before you set off on your reading journey, you need a map to show you where you are going – and you will have to make this map yourself. Ask yourself where you want to be at the end of your journey. Your answer to this question must be as specific as you can make it and tailored to the text you are reading and the course you are taking. Try not to answer the question of where you want to be by saying something like 'I want to know a bit about X or Y' or 'I have to broaden my knowledge of A or B.' Better replies would be 'The course requires a detailed knowledge of this process so I have a reading list to get me to that point' or 'I need to know this writer's opinion on X and I believe that this article will give me this.'

There are a number of things that must be taken into account when putting your map together:

▶ *An overview of your course. What are the main topics that you will have to master? Are some more important than others? Do you have examples of the assignments you will have to complete and copies of past examination papers?*

▶ *What are the planned learning outcomes for your course? If you are unsure about this, ask your tutor.*

▶ *Is there a recommended reading list? This list will have been put together by your tutors or the people who designed the course and it may or may not be thought necessary to read it in its entirety. It might be desirable to read all the books on the list but it will quite often not be possible and you will need to be selective about what you read.*

▶ What do you know already? *Is this a subject that you have already studied at some level? If so, you may have a different starting point with your reading map than someone who is coming to the subject with no knowledge at all.*

▶ Assignments you will have to complete – *compile a list of the topics which will be covered and the most likely exam questions – this will make your journey far more predictable.*

Insight

Don't forget to check the date of publication of any books and texts that you read to ensure that you are getting up-to-date information.

With your current level of knowledge as your starting point and the stated learning outcomes as your finishing point, you will need to plot your route through the topics to be covered. You will need to take into account the amount of time that you will be able to allocate to your journey and the assignments that you will have to cover – the stops along the way. It is at this point in developing your strategy that you will have to pay close attention to how you allot your available time for study to the various tasks you will have to undertake – of which reading is just one. If you have any doubt about how to do this, turn back to the section on time management in Chapter 2.

There are also more specific reading tasks and these also need to be planned. For example, if you are reading a number of articles to find alternative arguments to include in an essay, you will read differently to if you are trying to find just the right quote to finish that essay. If you are trying to gain an overview of a topic, then that will again be a different reading task. For each reading task you will need to ask questions such as the following to clarify your goals:

▶ *What information am I looking for?*
▶ *Is this information in the text I am about to read?*

- ▶ *How will I use this information?*
- ▶ *Do I need to remember this and in what level of detail?*
  Don't make the mistake of thinking that your goal in
  reading a text is to remember it. Your primary aim should
  always be to understand it and then to retain enough in
  your mind about the ideas that the author of the book
  or article is trying to get across. Making notes – active
  learning – *will usually help with this. If you can work with*
  the ideas, think about them and compare them with other
  views you may have read – *then you will have achieved one*
  of your reading goals.
- ▶ *Exactly how will reading this help me with the stated learning*
  outcomes? NB If you're not sure whether the article or book
  you are about to read will help you reach your goals, you must
  ask yourself why you're reading it.

Insight

Always have a goal when you're reading to study – if you
know what you are aiming for, you are far more likely to
achieve it.

Now, you've set yourself a strategy, know what you're aiming for
and how you're going to get there, but how will you carry out the
actual reading tasks?

Speed reading

Most students complain that they do not have time to read
everything that is expected of them. This is undoubtedly true and
it is necessary to be selective about what we read. We must read
the most important texts and maybe just skim the remainder so
that we understand what information is contained in them – more
about skimming later.

Even when we have pared down the amount we have to read, it
will still be important to read quickly, so how can we improve our

average reading speed? Here are a few things you can do to read more quickly:

▶ Get comfortable. *If you are relaxed when you sit down to read, your level of comprehension will improve and your reading speed will increase when you understand what you are reading.*

▶ Read with a purpose. *Decide what questions you want to answer from reading this particular text and ignore sections that do not add to this answer.*

▶ Focus on groups of words rather than on each individual word. *This will mean that your eyes will be jumping along the lines, resting on a few words at a time so that you understand the sense of the text without even seeing some of the words. By doing this, the number of times that your eyes pause and fix on a word will reduce and this will make the reading task quicker. With practice, you will find that not only do you get better at this but also you will stop noticing many of the smaller 'joining words' such as 'and', 'the', 'but' and 'because'. This will not affect the meaning of the sentences too much.*

▶ Notice words that will give you a clue as to the direction of the argument. *Words such as 'however', 'although' and 'nevertheless' signal that a change of ideas is imminent while words such as 'also', 'moreover' and 'in addition' let you know that the argument is being developed. A conclusion is usually signalled with words such as 'consequently', 'to sum up', 'therefore', 'thus' and, of course, 'in conclusion'.*

▶ Use a guide. *Moving your finger fairly quickly down the page (just keep your finger on one side of the text and move straight down – don't try to track every word as this will usually have the effect of slowing you down) can help you not only to keep your place in the text but also will speed you up as you try to keep pace with your finger. You could also try using a sheet of paper as a tracker.*

▶ Move your eyes forward continuously. *Lingering on a word or group of words will slow you down and interrupt your rhythm. Also going back in the text to check something that you might not quite have caught will slow you down considerably, so you will have to resist this temptation.*

- ▶ Don't move your lips! *Many people say the words to themselves as they read – or even read out loud – but this, too, will slow you down.*
- ▶ Practise. *Spend some time every day reading as fast as you can and you will soon improve your average speed.*

Improving your reading speed is essential to effective study so this is something that you should pay particular attention to. However, sometimes reading slowly is necessary too. It is not desirable to race through every bit of information that you are given to read as sometimes you will need to read more carefully than speed reading allows. This could include when you are reading a text with detailed instructions or really densely packed information. It would also include situations where you are required to closely analyse texts. So, work hard at increasing your average reading speed but remember that there will be times when it is more appropriate to read slowly.

You may be in the habit of quickly assessing the information in a text by checking the beginning and end and running your eye over the text. This is not speed reading; it is skimming. This is a very useful skill to have and in the next section we will look into how this is done.

Insight

Adjust your reading speed in line with the type of text you're reading and your aims in reading it.

Skimming

This is also known as selective reading and means that you do not read a book from cover to cover but simply select the bits that you need to read in order to find particular information or to judge whether or not the text is suitable for your purpose.

To skim a book, start with the front and back covers. The book title and subtitle will obviously tell you the subject matter contained in the book, while the back cover blurb will usually indicate the level of student at whom the book is aimed and more detail about what is covered in the book. Next, look at the contents page. If you do not find what you are looking for here, try the index.

Next you can start on the chapters. Perhaps from your check on the contents and index you will have decided that only one or two chapters are worthy of your time and attention. Read the first and last paragraphs of each of the chapters that interest you. This is where the main ideas and conclusions will usually be found. If there is a summary at the end of each chapter, read this too.

At this point you should have got a great deal of useful information out of a relatively small amount of reading. You will have gathered the main points and ignored the supporting facts and arguments that are often contained in the body of each paragraph. Sometimes, of course, it will be necessary for you to read the whole thing to find these supporting facts, but you will often find that skimming will produce sufficient information and save you spending hours reading a lot of detail. Alternatively, it can prove to you whether or not it will be worth your investing the time needed to read the whole text.

It is useful to make brief notes as you skim a text as it is easy to forget information acquired at this speed.

Insight

Even when you have decided that you should skim an article, keep an open mind and, if you find that there is a lot of useful information in the work, then be prepared to read the whole thing.

Active reading – developing a reading strategy

To read effectively and to put our reading time to the very best use possible, we must add an active element to it rather than letting the words flow over us. We need to engage with the text and make sure that we get just what we need from it. To do this we must ask questions continually and react to the answers. A word here about marking books. Unless the book is yours (and you find it acceptable to make marks in books – many people find it almost impossible to put even a pencil mark in the margins) you should not mark a book but make photocopies of relevant sections and then be interactive with those copies. Here are some of the questions that you should ask as you read:

▶ What is the main point of this book, chapter, essay or article? *Look for clues before you begin by checking the contents page, the back cover blurb or the title and sub-heading in the case of an article or essay.*

▶ What is the main idea in this paragraph? *This is usually contained in the first sentence or so. Highlight or underline the two or three words that encapsulate this idea.*

▶ Does this answer the questions that I have on this topic? *You should prepare a list of questions that you want to find the answers to before you start to read. If the text you're reading will not answer your questions, you are probably wasting your time and should move on to something else.*

▶ How does this compare with what I already know about this topic? *Is it introducing a different argument or adding to what I have already learned or maybe it contradicts what I thought was correct? You will have to decide, as you read, how this new information relates to your existing knowledge and how you will mesh this with current ideas. You may find that, if the viewpoint presented is not what you expected, you will have to do some further reading to ensure that you can present a balanced case.*

▶ Is the evidence valid and convincing? *In most academic texts, the author is making an argument and you will need to decide, in the light of what you already know and from the evidence the author presents, whether he or she has made their case.*

▶ What is the author's conclusion? *This will, of course, be in the final paragraph or chapter and you may find it useful to find it and underline it.*

Write down your questions and keep them by you as you read. To complete your active reading task, you will need to quickly reread the text, making notes as you go. Your underlinings or highlighting will help you in this, as they will draw you to the important points. By reading actively and interacting with the text, you will find it much easier to remember the useful bits.

Let's look at how this active reading works in practice by examining how we might deal with reading an article.

Exercise

Read the following text on choosing a training course, underlining or highlighting the answers to your questions as discussed earlier.

What is a good training course?
The answer to that question is simple – and complicated! Put simply, a good training course is one that meets all your requirements. Viewed in more depth, a good training course is one that will be effective – but defining that effectiveness can be quite difficult. You will need to do a lot of research so that you know what skills you already have within your organization and also that you know what training is available – and at what price – outside your company. When you have done this, you will then be in a position to choose your training. Use the checklist that follows to help.

Course choice checklist
▶ *Does the course content match the training need that you have identified? Will successful completion of the course enable your delegates to be able to do what you want them to do?*

▶ *Will the content keep your delegates interested? If you feel that they may be bored by parts of the material, take care – a bored delegate will not learn much and probably will not ultimately make a more effective employee.*

▶ *Is it going to be cost effective? i.e. will the benefits justify the costs?*

▶ *Does the course use the appropriate method of delivery? A course that is very practical and 'hands on' may not necessarily suit a* very academic subject with delegates who are senior managers in your organization. Similarly, a course based on listening and then completing written exercises may not be appropriate for practical skills training, with delegates who feel uncomfortable with written materials.

▶ Is the venue convenient and suitable? You must take into account possible costs of accommodation and travel as well as the size and layout of the training rooms.

▶ Is the course the right length? If it is an event of more than a day or two, can the business continue while the delegates are on the course? Will you have to organize temporary cover for any of the trainees' positions? Is the length appropriate for the subject matter?

▶ If you are considering an external course, do you know the training provider? If you have had previous, good experiences of the provider you are proposing to use, then you will be able to purchase a course with confidence. If you don't have personal experience of the training provider, do your research carefully.

▶ Does the course fit in with the culture of your organization? It may be that the training provider in question has a different approach to the subject from that of your business. For example, a course on disciplinary procedures may take a hard line towards minor transgressions. Managers returning from such a course to an organization with a much more lenient view of staff behaviour would find it difficult to put into practice what they have learned. This match between the culture of the organization and the approach of the training is important – unless your aim is to change your organization's culture, of course! In this case, the course will be just one part of your strategy for change.

Of course, any training solution that you decide on must meet the objectives set for the training at an affordable price. If you have neglected to set specific objectives, then you will be unable to tell whether the training course that you propose is going to be suitable, so read the earlier section about objectives and make that the very first thing you do after you have gathered all your information about the need for training in your organization.

(Contd)

Having set your objectives and obtained sufficient information about the training needs, you will be in a position to differentiate between a good course, i.e. one that is good quality and closely matches your needs, and a bad one.

From a delegate's point of view, a successful course is one that is not boring and that teaches them something useful. Obviously only the latter part of this view ties in directly with the objectives of the company paying for the training. However, it is essential that the delegate's needs are taken into account in assessing the effectiveness of a course. It is unlikely that a bored trainee will gain the maximum amount of usable knowledge from any training so the course should be structured so that the delegate's interest is maintained. A good training course will therefore contain a variety of different elements and learning methods.

How did you find that task? Did you get the gist of that short section of a book on training? Below is an example of the way you might have marked up the text. The text has been marked up by showing the key words and phrases in bold type. You might choose to underline or highlight the text.

Example

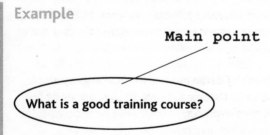

Main point

(**What is a good training course?**)

*The answer to that question is simple – and complicated! Put simply, a good training course is one that **meets all your requirements**. Viewed in more depth, a good training course is one that will be **effective** – but defining that effectiveness can be quite difficult. You will need to do a lot of research so that you know what skills you already have within your organization and also that you know what training is available – and at what price – outside your company. When you have done this, you will*

*then be in a position to choose your training. Use the checklist that
follows to help.*

Course choice checklist
*Does the course content **match the training need** that you have
identified? Will successful completion of the course enable your
delegates to be able to do what you want them to do?*

*Will the content **keep your delegates interested**? If you feel that they
may be bored by parts of the material, take care – a bored delegate will
not learn much and probably will not ultimately make a more effective
employee.*

*Is it going to be **cost effective**? i.e. will the benefits justify the costs?*

*Does the course use the **appropriate method of delivery**? A course that
is very practical and 'hands on' may not necessarily suit a very academic
subject with delegates who are senior managers in your organization.
Similarly, a course based on listening and then completing written exercises
may not be appropriate for practical skills training, with delegates who feel
uncomfortable with written materials.*

*Is the **venue convenient and suitable**? You must take into account
possible costs of accommodation and travel as well as the size and
layout of the training rooms.*

*Is the course the **right length**? If it is an event of more than a day or two,
can the business continue while the delegates are on the course? Will you
have to organize temporary cover for any of the trainees' positions? Is the
length appropriate for the subject matter?*

*If you are considering an external course, do you **know the training
provider**? If you have had previous, good experiences of the provider
you are proposing to use, then you will be able to purchase a course
with confidence. If you don't have personal experience of the training
provider, do your research carefully.*

(Contd)

*Does the course **fit in with the** culture of your organization? It may be that the training provider in question has a different approach to the subject from that of your business. For example, a course on disciplinary procedures may take a hard line towards minor transgressions. Managers returning from such a course to an organization with a much more lenient view of staff behaviour would find it difficult to put into practice what they have learned. This match between the culture of the organization and the approach of the training is important – unless your aim is to change your organization's culture, of course! In this case, the course will be just one part of your strategy for change.*

*Of course, any training solution that you decide on must **meet the objectives set for the training** at an affordable price. If you have neglected to set specific objectives, then you will be unable to tell whether the training course that you propose is going to be suitable, so read the earlier section about objectives and make that the very first thing you do after you have gathered all your information about the need for training in your organization.*

Having set your objectives and obtained sufficient information about the training needs, you will be in a position to differentiate between a good course, i.e. one that is good quality and closely matches your needs, and a bad one.

*From a delegate's point of view, a successful course is one that is not boring and that teaches them something useful. Obviously only the latter part of this view ties in directly with the objectives of the company paying for the training. However, it is essential that the delegate's needs are taken into account in assessing the effectiveness of a course. It is unlikely that a bored trainee will gain the maximum amount of usable knowledge from any training so the course should be structured to ensure the delegate's interest is maintained. A good training course will therefore contain a **variety of different elements and learning methods**.*

Conclusion?

Figure 3.1 Sample text markup.

If you go on to make notes on this text, using the bold words as your guide, you would, in this case, finish the task with a few notes on the subject. These can be laid out in a list:

Main point – what is a good training course?
Must meet all requirements and be effective
Match training need
Keep delegates interested
Be cost effective
Use appropriate method of delivery
Suitable venue
Right length
Check out provider
Does content fit our culture?
Set specific objectives for choosing a course
Conclusion – should contain a variety of different elements and learning
    methods

Now you must ask yourself whether you have learned sufficient information to answer the question 'What is a good training course?' or whether you may feel the need to look up different views on the subject. And finally, to check what you have learned, check how many of the points contained in the extract about choosing a course you can remember – without using your notes, of course. Having read, marked up and then made notes about a text, asking and answering questions as you go, you should find that you retain a significant amount of the information for which you were reading the text.

Now that you have learned about reading with a purpose, you need to find out some ways to record and retain the information you have obtained from your reading, so the next chapter is about note taking.

Quick revision test

1 *What is usually the first stage in academic reading?*
2 *When you are speed reading and have decided what questions you need to answer, what should you do about the sections that do not add to your answers?*
3 *Name two things that you could use as guides or trackers when speed reading.*
4 *Should you try to read everything as quickly as possible?*
5 *Name two places in a book where you might discover the main point of a book.*

10 THINGS TO REMEMBER

1 *Reading to learn is different from reading for pleasure – if you are to learn something then you will have to take an active approach.*

2 *Always set goals when reading to study.*

3 *Make sure any publications you read give you up-to-date information.*

4 *You will not have time to read everything that is expected of you, so be selective about what you read; take into account your starting point, the assignments you will have to complete along the way and the planned outcomes.*

5 *It is possible to improve your reading speed – by using a guide, looking for clues about the main points, and practice!*

6 *Skim a book to find the information that is important to you by checking the headings, introductions and summaries.*

7 *Active reading means that you must develop a reading strategy, including being clear about what you want to find out before you start to read; clarify your reading goals by asking questions of yourself such as what information you are looking for and how you will use it.*

8 *Reading is just one of the tasks that you have when you are studying and it is important that you allocate your time appropriately.*

9 *Although you will need to read most things quickly, make sure that you spend time on really important pieces of text.*

10 *Ask questions of yourself every time you read something and make sure that you have answered those questions when you have finished reading.*

4

....

Note taking

In this chapter you will learn:
- *why you need notes*
- *different ways of taking notes*
- *what to do with your notes.*

_____

When and why you need to take notes

Let's look first at the reasons why you might take notes. You may think that you have to take notes whenever and whatever you are learning because 'that's how things are'. But there are different situations in which you take notes and this may affect the style you choose to make your notes. Note taking is the traditional view of the student's work but it is not an end in itself, so when you're taking notes you need to be aware of the purpose of them. If you take a typical view of a student's work, it might mean that you make notes simply to prove to yourself – or to others – that you are working hard. They become the tangible evidence of your work rate. If you then abandon them in a pile on your desk, never to be looked at again, your work has been wasted. So, before you put pen or highlighter to paper or fingers to keyboard to take some notes, think carefully about why, exactly, you are making them.

One of the most common reasons for taking notes is to aid your memory. In this case, your notes will probably be brief jottings made as you read something or listen to a lecture. It is impossible for the vast majority of us to remember most of what we see or hear, so notes can be a useful way to store the facts and arguments we've learned so that we can use them later. Note making also helps us to assimilate the information. The act of writing down the most important points will help them to 'stick'.

Rather than general note taking of information for possible use later, you may be taking notes with a more specific purpose in mind. It may be that you are taking notes on a particular subject with the aim of gaining sufficient information to write an essay. Or perhaps you're making notes for exam revision. Another result of the act of note taking is that it helps you to understand what you are reading. If you have to put a complicated piece of text into your own words, you will understand it far better than if you simply read it.

Whatever the reason may be for taking the notes, it is important that you can find them and use them when necessary, so you must file them as soon as you can.

Insight

Before you start taking any notes, think about why you're taking them and what you will use them for. If you're not going to use them effectively there's no point in taking them.

Note taking in lectures

We're back to the traditional view of a student's work – sitting in a lecture writing down everything that the lecturer says. But, as we've seen before, that view is not a correct one – the student has to carry out many more tasks than note taking in lectures – and no one could be expected to write down everything someone said in a period of perhaps an hour or more. Note taking in lectures needs to be far more selective – and organized – than that.

Many people make the mistake that the sole purpose of a lecture is to provide material to be learned later, but there is far more to it than that and this affects the way lecture notes should be viewed. During a lecture or talk given by a tutor, your prime goal should be to make sense of what you are being told. Notes may be just one element that will help you to do this.

Having accepted that it will be impossible for you to write as quickly as someone speaks and also to let your brain engage with the ideas that are being put across, then you need to develop a strategy for note taking in lectures. In developing this strategy you will have to take into consideration the following:

▶ *Will there be any handouts to cover the contents of the lecture?*
▶ *Your way of working – do you usually take copious notes or are you a 'key points' person?*
▶ *Do you need to take notes to stop you from 'wandering off' into your own thoughts, i.e. to keep your concentration focused on the lecture?*

Your note-taking strategy for lectures should include, as a minimum, getting down on paper the broad structure of the lecture. The lecturer will often deal with this in the first few seconds of the session so make sure you're ready for it. At the other end of the lecture, the lecturer will usually summarize his or her thoughts and reach a conclusion, so this is another useful time to be giving your full concentration and making sure that you are getting it down on paper. To this outline you should aim to add at least a summary of the main points (in as much detail as you personally find necessary – don't forget that you need to be comfortable with the way of working) and also notes about the sources that the lecturer mentions. You may need to check out these sources for further information or to use them in assignments at a later date. If any questions occur to you during the lecture – maybe there is something you don't quite understand or see the significance of – then you should also jot these down. Making a note of the things you don't understand can be almost as important as noting the things you do understand. You can then ask questions after the lecture or go and find out the information for yourself in the library or in course books.

With the speed at which you will need to be making notes in lectures, you may not be able to pay much attention to the style you make them in, but do try to add some structure. Perhaps you will decide beforehand that any comments of your own will be made at the bottom of the page or to the left-hand side or you may get into the habit of using diagrammatic elements such as circling important points, adding arrows and lines to link relevant bits of information. You will also probably develop your own style of shorthand so that you will be able to take notes at speed but still be able to make sense of them later.

Some students use a recorder in lectures. While this might free you from the task of making notes during the lecture and allow you to focus your attention on listening and understanding, it is not a total solution. You will still need to decide how you will use these recorded notes. If you are very disciplined, and are prepared to invest your time not just in attending the lecture but also in going through the recordings later to make notes about the key points, then recording lectures can be an effective note-taking method. You will first, of course, need to check that the recording of lectures is acceptable to the lecturer.

Whichever way of note taking you choose to use in lectures, the most important point is that they should suit you and your way of working. They should be in a form that you can make effective use of at a later date.

Insight

It's important that you have a note-taking strategy during lectures – you need to get down the basics (including the sources mentioned by the lecturer) in a format that you are comfortable with.

Easy ways to take notes

When you're embarking on a course of study, you must be able to find easy ways to do everything – ways that make sense to you and will be in a format that will be useful to you in the future, but that aren't unnecessarily difficult or complicated or take ages to complete. Here are a few suggestions to make note taking easier:

▶ Highlight or underline the important bits – this is ideal for using on handouts or photocopied articles and so on. *Of course, you couldn't use this method in a book unless it was yours. It is a definite no-no for books you've borrowed. When using this method, you need to be able to pick out phrases of just a few words that sum up the main idea of a paragraph, and then you will use a highlighter pen (you may wish to use different colours to differentiate between different sorts of information) to make them stand out. Underlining will be used in exactly the same way and here again different coloured pens can be used. A word of advice, however – don't get carried away with your colour-coding system or you could end up spending more time on the system than the actual text.*

▶ Spider diagrams are another way of making note taking easy. *We will go into more detail as to how they can be made to work for you – with examples – in the next section, but, briefly, they are diagrams that start with the main idea in the middle and then radiate outwards with all the subsidiary ideas and information about a subject so that the finished article looks like a spider.*

▶ Many people develop their own shorthand system to speed up their note-taking process – especially when taking notes in lectures. *This could be something as simple as shortening words – for example, 'bcos' for 'because' or 'cd' for 'could' and using common abbreviations such as 'e.g.' instead of writing out 'for example' and 'i.e.' for 'that is'. If you decide to try this, it is worth remembering that our brains can interpret many words if we are given just the first and last letter or two – we can often ignore what's in the middle. Of course, if you are proficient at a recognized method of shorthand, you can use that but do make sure that you can read it easily. How awful it would be to make notes in shorthand and then, when you went back to your notes many weeks later, be unable to make sense of what you had written!*

How to take notes that work for you

However you decide to compile and file your notes, they must work for you. It is irrelevant that they may not make much sense to anyone else or not serve their purposes. Having decided what you will use the notes for, you must find an appropriate way to make the notes that fits in with the way you work and think. If you are a very creative, visual person, for example, having an element of illustration in the notes will be especially helpful. In this case, spider diagrams will be suitable, perhaps with little drawings added.

Look at Figure 4.1 overleaf; it shows how to make notes in the form of a spider diagram using the article from the active reading exercise in Chapter 3. As you can see, the main idea – this could be the subject of an assignment or an article you have to read – has been placed in the centre of the paper and all subsidiary ideas radiate out from this – making a drawing that looks a bit like a spider or, if you make lots of connections, like a series of spiders all joined up. This is a good way to brainstorm an idea as each thing that occurs to you can be added to the diagram and will usually spark off your thoughts, so that eventually you will have written down most of what you know about the central idea. It is also an effective way of making the links in a subject that will clarify your understanding of it and will improve your ability to remember it.

Of course, spiders are not the only way to make notes that incorporate visual elements. You could also use different coloured pens and highlighters, or make notes in the form of a pyramid (with the topic at the top and different sub-headings forming the lower levels, 'drilling down' into the topic until you have the amount of detail you need). Perhaps you could add asterisks or other symbols to draw attention to different elements. These methods are ideal examples of active learning and will help you to understand and recall important information.

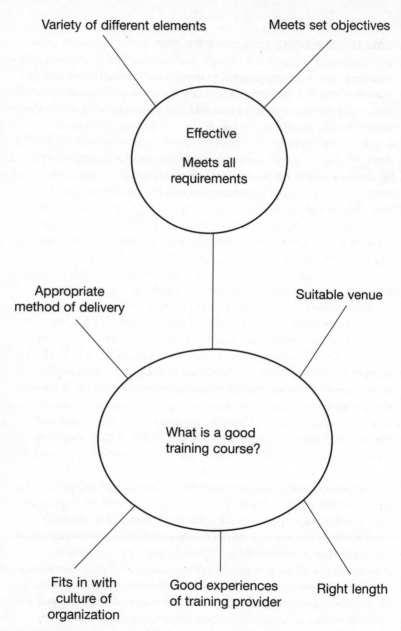

Variety of different elements   Meets set objectives

Effective

Meets all
requirements

Appropriate
method of delivery   Suitable venue

What is a good
training course?

Fits in with
culture of
organization   Good experiences
of training provider   Right length

Figure 4.1 Making notes using a spider diagram.

If, however, you like to use your auditory senses, you could make audiotapes of your main notes and perhaps play them to yourself over and over again. Even though you may find that your mind wanders off a bit during tapes, you will still absorb plenty of the information, as it will wander off at a different point each time you listen and, sooner or later, you will have listened to the whole thing with full concentration.

Another way that you can tailor your notes to your learning style is to use carefully written notes if you have a visual style. Here you might make notes during a lecture or while reading an article and then review them to make them more succinct. Pick out the few words (as few as you can) that sum up the ideas and arguments contained in the notes and write them down – index cards, one per topic, are useful for this.

Insight

Make notes in a way that suits you and your learning style. There are many different ways of making notes so find one that is right for you.

Although you will have plenty of freedom as to the style of your note taking, there are a few things that you definitely should not do when you are taking notes:

▶ Do not write down every word said in a lecture – *this could be next to impossible anyway but would mean that you were not paying real attention to what was being said. You need to give your mind time to recognize, organize and reorganize the material as you go along.*
▶ Do not copy whole chunks of a book or article – *this will be boring and may also mean that you have not fully understood the sense of the work.*
▶ Don't crowd everything together – *leave some white space (wide margins, spaces between the lines and so on) around all your notes as this will make them not only more visually pleasing but also easier to read. This applies whether you're hand writing your notes or compiling them with the help of a computer.*

- Don't copy out your notes simply to make them look nice. *Unless you're using the rewriting as an exercise to revise or get to grips with the material, but you already have got a legible set of notes, don't waste time copying them out.*
- Don't take notes that you don't need. *If you don't believe that you will use the notes,* don't make them.

Now that you know what not to do with your notes and you've learned a few ways to make notes that work for you, here are a few things that you should do as you compile them:

- **Make sure you have understood what you have read or heard before you write anything.** *Think about what you are writing so that you can identify the main ideas of what you are learning – the main ideas are what you should be noting.*
- **Keep them short** *– many students take copious notes that are daunting to read so they are put in a pile and never looked at again. Keep them short, relevant and useful.*
- **Use plenty of headings and sub-headings** *– these not only break up the text, making it easier to read, but also will enable you to find just what you're looking for in the future.*
- **Put everything into your own words** *– this will make the act of note taking more beneficial to you in that you will have to think about the information you are dealing with as you rephrase and summarize it.*
- **Listen and look out for clues to the important bits.** *If, for example, a text (or a lecturer) says 'The three most significant stages are …' then you need to note the three things that follow.*
- **Use abbreviations** *and make sure that you write key words and phrases rather than copying out whole sentences.*
- **Organize your thoughts as you write** *– this will result in organized notes and will also mean that you will understand (and hopefully remember) what you have written.*
- **Write important bits** *– perhaps a quotation (and its source, of course) or a useful phrase that you want to remember exactly – in a different colour.*
- **Remember** *– you must have a purpose to your note taking. Know why you are making the notes and what question they will answer for you.*

- ▶ *Vary your approach* so that on some occasions you will take detailed notes and on others very brief notes. The main thing is that they must be doing the job you want them to do.
- ▶ *Note what you haven't understood.* This is just as important as what you have understood. Make sure you ask questions at the first opportunity if you feel you've not understood an important point.

Insight

If you think that you may quote from your notes at some later stage, make sure that you make a note of the source of the quotation.

What to do with your notes

Unless you develop a way of making sure that your notes are easy to find when you need them, you will have wasted most of the time you spent on making them (although note making always has some benefit as it is active learning) so you will need to get hold of some files and folders and make some space on the shelves in your study area so that you can store them efficiently. Ring binders are especially useful as this will enable you to use dividers to separate the different topic areas and to add or extract notes as and when required.

It is unrealistic to think that you will ever sit down and read your notes through from start to finish at some time in the future, so filing them in topic areas (rather than as a subject from start to finish) will probably be the most useful to you. In this way you will be able to find the information you need for an assignment, when preparing for a lecture or when revising for examinations.

Insight

You'll find a contents page at the front of your notes file useful. Update it each time you add to your notes.

Apart from getting your notes organized, what else should you do with them? How will you use them? As we've already said, you probably won't read them through again. Rather than reading them – which is a passive way of using your notes – you need to be active with them. You need to change them in some way that will help you to understand them while you are working on them and will also help you to remember them in the longer term. Ways of working with your notes – especially if they are linear notes (notes where everything is written down in the order in which it is said or read – line by line) could include:

▶ Condensing them – *this is almost self-explanatory. You're making them shorter. To do this you might pick out the key words from your notes.*
▶ Creating a different type of notes – *consider converting your linear notes into a spider diagram.*
▶ Recording the key words – *if your learning style (we dealt with this in Chapter 2) is auditory, i.e. you learn best by using your sense of hearing, then recording the most important and relevant bits of your notes on to audiotapes could provide a valuable revision aid.*
▶ Use them for another purpose – *perhaps you could set yourself an exam-type question and write for 30 or 40 minutes using only the information contained in the notes. This has three distinct benefits:*
   1 *You will be using and digesting your notes so that you will definitely remember more from them in the future.*
   2 *You will be giving yourself valuable practice in essay writing or question answering to time limits.*
   3 *You will be able to see whether or not your notes were sufficiently detailed – or too detailed.*

Using technology to help with note taking

If you're making and keeping notes on your computer, your approach will be very similar to note taking manually – you will need to keep them short and relevant, make them with a purpose in mind and keep them organized. It is this last aspect of computerized note taking where you will see some differences and will see a benefit from using technology.

It is vital that all files stored on a computer are named and then filed in the right place. If you are careless about naming and filing your files, your computer will become like an enormous desk, overflowing with loose papers. You will waste endless hours searching for that one elusive file that you know is there somewhere but you can't recall where you put it or what you called it. If you do find yourself in that situation, try performing a search based on the approximate date when you worked on the file in question. The best idea, however, is not to get into that sort of difficulty. Follow these tips for organizing your computer files:

▶ *Name your file and decide where you will store it as soon as you create a new file.*
▶ *Choose your file name carefully. The name should tell you what is in the file so make sure you include, at a minimum, the topic covered in the file.*
▶ *Use folders and sub-folders to store your files. For instance, you may have a folder named 'Course XXX' that contains sub-folders named 'Notes', 'Assignments' and 'Research' and within those sub-folders you will have sub-sub-folders with titles based on the topics covered in the files. The important thing is to have a path of folders and files that makes sense to you and that you can follow until it leads you to exactly what you are looking for.*
▶ *Keep files small. It may be tempting to put all your notes for your entire course in one file so that you know where they are, but you will find it time-consuming and frustrating to page up and down through a very long file to find the section of these notes that covers the topic you're interested in.*

Insight

Make a backup copy of all your files – this applies to assignments as well as your notes. If something goes wrong, you may find that your notes are irreplaceable.

Quick revision test

1 *Give two general reasons for taking notes.*
2 *Give two specific purposes for which you may take notes.*
3 *What should you take into consideration when developing a strategy for note taking in lectures?*
4 *Where will the main idea be placed in a spider diagram?*
5 *Name a passive way and an active way of using your notes.*

10 THINGS TO REMEMBER

1 *The most important thing about note taking is that you use them later – if you're not going to use them, don't take them.*

2 *Find a way of taking notes that suits you and your learning style.*

3 *Always have a strategy for taking notes in lectures. Know why and how you're going to take them.*

4 *Find a way of taking notes that you find easy whether it is summarising key ideas, highlighting or underlining key words and phrases, your own shorthand or formulating a spider diagram – don't struggle with a style that doesn't work for you.*

5 *Keep notes short and easy to read.*

6 *Don't copy out your notes just to make them look nice.*

7 *When note taking put everything into your own words – this will help with understanding the work as you go along.*

8 *If there's something you don't understand during note taking, make a note of it and look it up or ask questions as soon as you can.*

9 *Use your notes in different ways – condense them, put them into a different style, use them for revision or for answering exam-style questions. This can help to develop your understanding of the topic.*

10 *Keep your notes organized.*

5

Thinking critically

In this chapter you will learn:
- *how to distinguish between opinions and facts*
- *how to evaluate an argument*
- *how to draw your own conclusions from your studying.*

Taking a critical approach to academic texts

When studying at a higher level, it is not sufficient to read, take notes and then repeat the information in assignments or examinations. You must develop a more critical approach to your studies. You will be required to evaluate the arguments that are presented to you and to see how the evidence presents a case both for and against a hypothesis. This is critical thinking and is an essential skill to master as it will help you to understand the material you read and to produce written work at the right level.

Of course, getting proficient at critical thinking will not happen overnight. It is a skill that will build as you practise. When you're first reading an academic text you will read it to understand the author's point of view. You will then try to find the arguments and check whether – and, indeed, where – you have met these arguments before. You will search for the evidence that the author puts forward to justify his or her arguments. You may then need to read the work of other authors to give you opposing or similar views. Your task then is to decide whether a strong enough case for the original arguments has been made and which view you are finding the most persuasive. It sounds like a lot of work – and of course, it can be – but, as you become more active in your reading tasks and develop your critical thinking capabilities, you will find it becomes easier over time.

All academic texts will put forward a view and, apart from understanding and remembering that view, your task will, as we saw previously, include evaluating the evidence given to justify it. You will need to decide whether or not the view being taken is reasonable and logical, given the evidence in the text and also the information that you already have at your disposal. The author of an academic text will explain his or her ideas by way of arguments and examples to illustrate the view taken. As you read it, you will be evaluating the arguments for and against the view taken by the author and deciding whether or not to accept the author's assertions. If the reasons, arguments and evidence are strong enough, you will be convinced by the conclusion drawn by the author at the end of the piece.

Insight

Understanding the arguments in any piece of work that you read is the first step in thinking critically.

Finding the arguments

Now that you can see why you will be looking for arguments and points of view to evaluate, you might be wondering whether or not you will be able to find these arguments. In almost every academic text that you have to read there will be a line of reasoning and the way you will identify this is by asking questions as you read. You will not be able to take any assertion as a fact unless you have asked yourself what, why, when, where and how? An argument can appear as:

▶ *A line of reasoning.*
▶ *A case being made.*
▶ *A point of view.*
▶ *A position being taken.*

In all cases, the author will put forward reasons – evidence and examples – why you should accept his or her argument. Your job is to find this argument, i.e. what they are saying about the subject of their text and whether they are taking a positive or negative view.

Insight

It is always useful to underline text or use a highlighter pen when you're looking for arguments – but only if you own the books and articles you're using, of course.

Here's an exercise that will help you to find arguments and points of view in a text:

Exercise

Read the following text and see if you can find the arguments in it.

'Philip Larkin – just a grumpy old man – or England's moral conscience and national poet?'

The contents of Philip Larkin's poems are no doubt the cynical rantings of a 'grumpy old man', but it is Larkin's talent in expressing these ideas that makes his pessimistic view of English life so convincing. We are often led to agree with the poet in what he is saying, not because of a predisposition to cynicism or discontent, but because he manages to put his views across so interestingly and concisely. Looking at the five poems separately, we see that each varies in its success in expressing one of Larkin's many dissatisfactions with British society. I believe the success of each usually depends on the tone that he uses.

In 'Wires', Larkin uses the image of cattle to symbolize humans and the transition they go through in life, from innocence in youth to experience. 'Young steers are always scenting purer waters' is meant to mirror the fact that young people believe that anything is possible for them, but soon find out that this is not the case, as their futures are much more predestined than they believe. Larkin employs subtle devices in 'Wires' to gently press his point across. His use of a cyclical structure, where the first line rhymes with the last line, gives the feeling of inevitability and endlessness to his perception that growing up is realizing that there are boundaries to our aspirations, and that this must happen to every generation: 'Electric limits to their widest senses'. He uses the shocking image of 'muscle-shredding violence' to mark the day of realization that our range of choice and possibility is actually very limited.

Larkin is successful with 'Wires' in that he manages to express a key perception about English society in a total of three sentences. As the language and construction that he uses are both basic, the poignancy of the message is not hidden or diluted, instead remaining plain and truthful.

Compared with 'Wires', 'Going, Going' is much less successful. The effect of this poem is to show Larkin as simply discontented and nostalgic, rather than perceptive. His aggressive, didactic tone is also unappealing as it makes him appear a constantly negative critic rather than a neutral spectator. His disapproval of everything, rather than some particular things, gives his overall message less weight as he has been so offensive in making it. Larkin's comparison between old and new England is so exaggerated as to make his point practically invalid. His nostalgic fantasy of the England of times past, 'The shadows, the meadows, the lanes, the guildhalls, the carved choirs', is far too idealistic, as it fails to recognize the bad sides of life at that time.

Although Philip Larkin may be making a point that some people agree with, he is not effective in expressing his idea in a way that most people can relate to, as his approach is so pessimistic and satirical. For me, it is this poem that best shows Larkin as a 'grumpy old man', as he fails to make the poem appeal to the moral conscience of the nation because he insults them so much, calling them 'a cast of crooks and tarts'.

(Contd)

'Annus Mirabilis' is similar to 'Wires' in its approach. The tone is casual and rather comical, in fact. Rather than a long rambling fatalistic rant, 'Annus Mirabilis' is short and light hearted, with a message that allows us to see the dawning of the sexual revolution as both a good and bad thing. It was good, in that it made life more fun and enjoyable, but negative in that it meant people lost the sense of responsibility for their actions. In this poem, Larkin presents a much more equal argument – recognizing that 1963 was a year of enjoyment and promiscuity but also commenting that it was a gamble, as no game is completely 'unloseable'.

'Annus Mirabilis' is unlike 'Wires' or 'Going, Going' as it actually claims that things might have got better since the past in some ways! Larkin writes, 'Up until then there'd only been A sort of bargaining, A wrangle for a ring, A shame that started at sixteen.' He then contrasts this with 1963, when 'every life became A brilliant breaking of the bank, A quite unloseable game'.

In 'This Be the Verse', Larkin gives voice to a controversial concept. In his era, parents were to be respected and obeyed, not insulted. Although the title of the poem has religious connotations, the sentiments that he writes about are deeply irreligious: first, because of foul language ('They fuck you up'), second, because the Bible teaches that you must 'Honour your mother and father', and, third, because we are meant to 'Go forth and multiply' (instead Larkin suggests you 'don't have any kids yourself'). The irreverent tone of the poem makes it funny and catchy as well as being cynical and nihilistic. It is the fact that the poem does not take itself too seriously that makes the message more appealing.

'High Windows' reverts mildly back to the 'Going, Going' tone of emphasizing the transition made by every generation away from that of their parents. He shows the way that each new generation discards something that their parents valued – in the case of these 'kids', it is 'Bond and gestures pushes to one side Like an outdated combine harvester'. He also uses the word 'fucking' to imply that it is sex without emotion or bonds. It is strange that he uses the image of going 'down the long slide to happiness' – an unusual way of putting it, as happiness is normally seen to be a journey upwards, and downwards as a decline in morality or *values. Perhaps by this he is commenting that happiness comes when we forget traditions and manners, and succumb to hedonism: sex without responsibility, and life without imposed religion. By questioning whether the generation before him looked at him with disapproval, he is accepting the inevitability of change in society.*

The last paragraph is in an entirely different tone to the colloquial familiarity of the first four stanzas. The lingering, transcendent image of 'high windows' is an ambiguous ending to the poem, perhaps suggesting that all we see is our own small sections of the world, like high windows from below, and that what we see is tiny compared with the whole picture. This could be saying that it is easy to be small minded but that instead we should be open to different ways of living. Alternatively it could be saying that our freedom should be framed with convention: our freedom being the 'deep blue air' beyond, and the bonds to it being like windows.

So, in deciding whether Philip Larkin is really just a 'grumpy old man' or is our national conscience, we must look at how effective his poems are. I believe that he is usually extremely skilled in expressing his (often depressing) views and it is these poems that really work. It is when his own sense of moral superiority overtakes that Larkin writes poems that elicit no empathy of agreement in the reader.

Did you immediately spot that the line of reasoning the author adopts here is that Larkin's ideas succeed, not because they are necessarily right, but because he is so skilled in putting them into words? Or did it take you some time to identify it? There are several assumptions that you should have been questioning as you read the piece and we will be looking more closely at these in the next section when we evaluate the arguments. If you are in any doubt as to the main point of the text, go through it again, this time with a highlighter pen or (especially if this book is not yours) a pen and paper. Highlight or note down the key words in the piece. You should end up with something like Figure 5.1. In this example the text has been marked up by showing the key words and phrases in bold type. You might choose to underline or highlight your text.

'Philip Larkin – just a grumpy old man – or England's moral conscience and national poet?'

The contents of Philip Larkin's poems are no doubt the cynical rantings of a 'grumpy old man', but it is **Larkin's talent in expressing these ideas** *that makes his pessimistic view of English life so convincing. We are often led to agree with the poet in what he is saying, not because of a predisposition to cynicism or discontent, but* **because he manages to put his views across so interestingly and concisely.** *Looking at the five poems separately, we see that each varies in its success in expressing one of Larkin's many dissatisfactions with British society. I believe the success of each usually depends on the tone that he uses.*

In 'Wires', Larkin uses the image of cattle to symbolize humans and the transition they go through in life, from innocence in youth to experience. 'Young steers are always scenting purer waters' is meant to mirror the fact that young people believe that anything is possible for them, but soon find out that this is not the case, as their futures are much more predestined than they believe. Larkin employs **subtle devices** *in 'Wires'* **to gently press his point** *across. His use of a cyclical structure, where the first line rhymes with the last line, gives the feeling of inevitability and endlessness to his perception that growing up is realizing that there are boundaries to our aspirations, and that this must happen to every generation: 'Electric limits to their widest senses'. He uses the shocking image of 'muscle-shredding violence' to mark the day of realization that our range of choice and possibility is actually very limited.*

Larkin is successful with 'Wires' in that he manages **to express a key perception about English society in a total of three sentences.** *As the language and construction that he uses are both basic, the poignancy of the message is not hidden or diluted, instead remaining plain and truthful.*

Compared with 'Wires', 'Going, Going' is much less successful. The effect of this poem is to show Larkin as simply discontented and nostalgic, rather than perceptive. **His aggressive, didactic tone is also unappealing** *as it makes him appear a constantly negative critic rather than a neutral* spectator. His **disapproval of everything**, rather than some particular things, **gives his overall message less weight** as he has been so offensive in making it. Larkin's comparison between old and new England is so **exaggerated** as to make his **point practically invalid**. His nostalgic fantasy of the England of times past, 'The shadows, the meadows, the lanes, the guildhalls, the carved choirs', is far too idealistic, as it **fails** to recognize the bad sides of life at that time.

Although Philip Larkin may be making a point that some people agree with, he is not effective in expressing his idea in a way that most people can relate to, as his approach is so pessimistic and satirical. For me, it is this poem that best shows **Larkin as a 'grumpy old man'**, as he **fails to make the poem appeal** to the moral conscience of the nation because he insults them so much, calling them 'a cast of crooks and tarts'.

'Annus Mirabilis' is similar to 'Wires' in its approach. The tone is casual and rather comical, in fact. Rather than a long rambling fatalistic rant, 'Annus Mirabilis' is short and light hearted, with a message that allows us to see the dawning of the sexual revolution as both a good and bad thing. It was good, in that it made life more fun and enjoyable, but negative in that it meant people lost the sense of responsibility for their actions. In this poem, Larkin presents a **much more equal** argument – recognizing that 1963 was a year of enjoyment and promiscuity but also commenting that it was a gamble, as no game is completely 'unloseable'.

'Annus Mirabilis' is unlike 'Wires' or 'Going, Going' as it actually claims that things might have got better since the past in some ways! Larkin writes, 'Up until then there'd only been A sort of bargaining, A wrangle for a ring, A shame that started at sixteen.' He then contrasts this with 1963, when 'every life became A brilliant breaking of the bank, A quite unloseable game'.

In 'This Be the Verse', Larkin gives voice to a controversial concept. In his era, parents were to be respected and obeyed, not insulted. Although the title of the poem has religious connotations, the sentiments that he writes about are deeply irreligious: first, because of foul language ('They fuck you up'), second, because the Bible teaches that you must 'Honour
(Contd)

your mother and father', and, third, because we are meant to 'Go forth and multiply' (instead Larkin suggests you 'don't have any kids yourself'). The irreverent tone of the poem makes it funny and catchy as well as being cynical and nihilistic. It is the fact that the poem **does not take itself too seriously that makes the message more appealing**.

'High Windows' reverts mildly back to the 'Going, Going' tone of emphasizing the transition made by every generation away from that of their parents. He shows the way that each new generation discards something that their parents valued – in the case of these 'kids', it is 'Bond and gestures pushes to one side Like an outdated combine harvester'. He also uses the word 'fucking' to imply that it is sex without emotion or bonds. It is strange that he uses the image of going '**down the long slide** to happiness' – an unusual way of putting it, as happiness is normally seen to be a journey upwards, and downwards as a decline in morality or values. Perhaps by this he is commenting that happiness comes when we forget traditions and manners, and succumb to hedonism: sex without responsibility, and life without imposed religion. By questioning whether the generation before him looked at him with disapproval, he is accepting the inevitability of change in society.

The last paragraph is in an entirely different tone to the colloquial familiarity of the first four stanzas. The lingering, transcendent image of 'high windows' is an ambiguous ending to the poem, perhaps suggesting that all we see is our own small sections of the world, like high windows from below, and that what we see is tiny compared with the whole picture. This could be saying that it is easy to be small minded but that instead we should be open to different ways of living. Alternatively it could be saying that our freedom should be framed with convention: our freedom being the 'deep blue air' beyond, and the bonds to it being like windows.

So, in deciding whether Philip Larkin is really just a 'grumpy old man' or is our national conscience, we must look at how effective his poems are. I believe that he is usually extremely skilled in expressing his (often depressing) views, and it is these poems that really work. It is when his own sense of moral superiority overtakes that Larkin writes poems that elicit no empathy of agreement in the reader.

From this highlighted piece, it should become more obvious to you that the main argument being put forward by the author of this piece is that Larkin's ideas carry more weight when he writes a poem with the right tone. The writer believes that, to be convincing, Larkin must suppress his tendency to act like a 'grumpy old man' and to write to gain the agreement of his reader.

The writer of this critique of Larkin's work backs up this argument with a consistent and logical review of how several of his poems work – or don't work – and why.

This essay was written by an unnamed student and as we do not know who the writer is or anything about his or her background, we are unable to evaluate whether there is any hidden agenda in the work. If, for example, we knew that it had been written by a competitor of Larkin's, then we might assume a motive other than a straightforward critique with nothing to gain apart from marks for a college assignment. However, we can deduce that the argument was put together by someone who has studied and, in the main, enjoyed Larkin's work and is not imposing a political view on it.

The evidence that is produced in the essay is directly related to the work and, of course, anyone wishing to confirm any of the quotes and so on could simply look up the poems. However, even this straightforward evidence should not be taken at face value. Many of the assertions made are opinion and may not be fact. This is a good example of where it may be useful to read another view. Someone else might not find Larkin's tone in his poem 'Going, Going' 'aggressive and didactic'. They might find the tone forceful and instructive and, of course, the tone is an important part of the writer's view. It is the tone that the writer perceives that is central to the argument put forward.

Although the arguments in this piece are often just the writer's opinions, they are, nonetheless, put forward logically and consistently.

Evaluating arguments

Now that you've found the arguments, you have to evaluate them –
weigh up the evidence for and against the idea that the author is
putting across in the text. There are a number of decisions you
have to make about the arguments and different ways to look
at the material. Use this checklist to evaluate the arguments you
found in the piece about Larkin's work:

▶ *Who is making this argument? Would they have anything to
gain by putting forward erroneous arguments?*
▶ *Where are they coming from? Is the author writing from a
noticeable point of view – is he coming politically from the
left or the right, for example?*
▶ *Is the argument relevant?*
▶ *Is it logical?*
▶ *Is the argument carried through logically?*
▶ *What evidence in support of the argument is included in
the text?*
▶ *Is this evidence reliable? What sources have been used?*
▶ *Are the argument and its supporting evidence consistent?*
▶ *Do you know of any evidence against the argument?*
▶ *Have you heard this argument before? If so, where?*
▶ *Have you read an opposing view anywhere? If so, where?*
▶ *Does this argument support what you already knew?*
▶ *Is the reasoning sound – or flawed?*
▶ *If numerical data is used to make the case, has it been
collected under fair conditions?*
▶ *Does the case that has been made fully support the conclusion
reached by the author?*

Insight
Note the main points of any evaluation – is the argument
logical, relevant, well reasoned and with plenty of supporting
evidence?

Drawing conclusions

Do you agree with the author's conclusions? At this point, you should have evaluated the evidence and reached your own conclusion as to whether or not the author has made his or her case. Did the case convince you? If so, why and how?

The author's conclusions will normally come at the end of the piece and it is worthwhile to underline, highlight or jot down exactly what that conclusion is. You might like to do this on your first read-through of the text so that you can then check out whether the evidence supports it and whether the author makes a sufficiently strong case to convince you that his or her point of view is the right one. Reading in this way is reading critically or analytically and can be time-consuming but is necessary when reading academic texts for a course of study. It is important that you do not merely accept an author's argument at face value. You must delve deeper and evaluate the evidence given (and the evidence not given) to prove or disprove the case.

Insight

When you're evaluating an argument, make sure that you consider not only the evidence given but also anything you may know that would contradict the argument that has been left out. Sometimes, things that are left out are the most telling.

Using a critical approach in your writing

At the same time as you are mastering the skill of thinking critically when you are reading, you will also be working on your writing skills – academic writing requires you to present arguments and then justify them with evidence in much the same way as the texts you have been reading. If you follow a step-by-step approach to this, you will find that the standard of your academic essays, reports and dissertations will be substantially increased:

1 Decide on your main argument – *your most important line of reasoning should run through your essay or other written work. Further arguments will be needed to add weight to your main one.*

2 Gather the evidence – *you will gather lots of evidence at the research stage of your essay writing but you must then be selective about which pieces of evidence you use. Too many will obscure your case and make the essay difficult to read and understand, so make sure that you choose the most convincing ones and that they clearly support your main line of reasoning.*

3 Consider other points of view – *how could someone argue against your case? If you have considered this as you write, your work will be much clearer and more convincing. You need to look at your arguments objectively so that you can consider not just the strengths but also the weaknesses in your case. If you can see a weakness and perhaps see that another writer could make a completely opposite case, you should try to deal with this in your essay. Make the evidence for your main line of reasoning stronger and also bring the opposing view into your essay with evidence that you have found against it. Balance the weaknesses you find with strong evidence.*

4 Reach a clear conclusion – *this is most important. If your conclusion is not clear, your whole essay will lose its impact. From the very first words of your introductory paragraph and through all your arguments, the writing should be leading towards your conclusion. Your readers should be in no doubt as to what your conclusion is. It is a good idea to write down your conclusion as soon as you have decided what it will be – perhaps this will be early on in your research when you have just started to gather evidence – and you may need to refine it along the way, but knowing your conclusion will give you a better chance of producing a coherent piece of work.*

5 Review your work – *a quick read-through is not enough for critical writing and thinking. Such a process may just find a*

few grammatical errors or spot the need for a bit of rewriting here and there. With critical thinking, a deeper evaluation is necessary. You will need to ask yourself questions such as:

▷ *Is my main argument clear?*
▷ *Have I produced sufficient evidence to back it up?*
▷ *Have I got specifics – names, dates, numerical data, sources and so on?*
▷ *Have I put this argument in both the introduction and the conclusion?*
▷ *Is any of my reasoning flawed?*
▷ *What are the strengths and weaknesses of my case?*
▷ *Is the conclusion clear?*

If you can follow these steps and answer these questions, you should be able to produce an essay – or other work – that will earn you good marks.

Insight

When you've finished a piece of academic writing, read it through and make sure that your argument is logical and runs through the entire piece, culminating in a conclusion.

Quick revision test

1 *Name three ways that an argument may appear in an academic text.*
2 *What will an author of an academic text use to convince you that their main line of reasoning is correct?*
3 *Where does a conclusion usually appear in an academic essay and what should you do when you find it?*
4 *Without which very important feature will an academic essay have less impact?*
5 *What are the five steps to the construction of a good critical essay?*

10 THINGS TO REMEMBER

1   *It is essential to take an analytical approach to academic texts; read, understand and critically evaluate, don't just accept everything you read at face value.*

2   *You must ask questions as you read, for example who is making the case, is it relevant and logical, is the evidence reliable, how does the argument fit in with what you already know, is the reasoning sound or flawed?*

3   *When you read you are looking for the author's line of reasoning.*

4   *It is useful to underline or highlight the argument and the main evidence as you read.*

5   *Any argument in an academic piece of work must be logical and well reasoned.*

6   *There must always be a clear conclusion when an argument is presented in a piece of work.*

7   *Sufficient evidence must be used to back up the argument.*

8   *Sources of any evidence must be given.*

9   *A review of the finished work is essential to make sure that the argument is logical and supported by evidence and that the conclusion is clear.*

10 *Consider the author's background – if it is known – when evaluating an argument. This may inform you about their starting position, political views, etc.*

6

Research skills

In this chapter you will learn:
- *how to develop your research skills*
- *how to explore two different resources for your research.*

Finding out what you need to research

If you're a fairly new student or if things have changed beyond recognition since you last studied seriously (after all, the Internet has become widely used only in the last few years), then you may be wondering exactly what you should be researching and how to go about it. But don't be worried by having to research. It is not some mysterious function of an academic, locked away somewhere in a dusty university library. It is simply about increasing your knowledge by reading and investigating and is a study skill that can be learned and improved.

Research information and its sources are often classified as either 'primary' or 'secondary'. To explain the difference, let's look at where you might find primary or secondary data, i.e. the sources.

Primary sources could include:

▶ Original documentation – *treaties, birth, death and marriage certificates.*

- ▶ Your own data – *if you carry out an interview, experiment or questionnaire you will produce primary data.*
- ▶ What you see for yourself – *you might observe behaviour in animals or in people that you would use as primary data.*
- ▶ Case studies – *accounts of real-life scenarios.*
- ▶ Original materials – *such as books, films and television programmes could be primary sources in the case of literature or media studies.*

Secondary sources could include:

- ▶ Literature – *most of the academic texts, books and articles that you will use in your studies.*
- ▶ Other people's data – *observations, experiments and questionnaires carried out by someone else will be secondary data to you.*

Having read the lists of primary and secondary sources, you will be able to see that the difference between the two is originality. If it is first hand to you it will be primary data, whereas if it is 'second hand' – i.e. the result of someone else's research, arguments and opinions and the criticism of original data – then it will be classed as being from a secondary source.

When you have to undertake research you will have a specific purpose. You will need to increase your knowledge in a particular area. For example, you may have an assignment to complete and need to find out more about the subject matter. In this case, don't rush to the library and get all the books remotely related to the assignment topic or go on to the Internet and search vaguely for hours for something relevant. You need to work smarter than that. You need to plan.

Your first step if you are researching for an assignment – say, an essay – should be to evaluate the assignment carefully. Ask yourself the following questions:

- ▶ What is the question? *Analyse the question so that you know what is really being asked.*
- ▶ How many words are required? *This will help you to assess how deeply you need to research the topic. If you have only*

250 words to write, then you will not be able to go into too much detail in your assignment. If, on the other hand, you are writing a dissertation of 25,000 words, then you will have to research the topic much more thoroughly.

▶ Is the question a regular one? *If the same question is asked every year on this course, then it is likely that you will already have studied what you need to put into the essay (may be you've got a handout about it) and will need to do only a bit of research to find one or two pieces of evidence to back up the argument.*

▶ Is the question pointing you to a particular article or book? *If it's about a recent event or new research, then the area to research can be narrowed.*

▶ How much time do you have? *If the deadline for the assignment is imminent, you will have to tailor your research very carefully. If, on the other hand, you have planned your timetable well and allowed yourself some time for the necessary research, you will be able to read around the subject.*

▶ Can you find out how the assignment will be marked? *If it's split into various parts, then you will be able to allocate your research time accordingly.*

Insight

Always get an idea of how much research will be necessary to complete your assignment before you start to research and plan accordingly.

Right, now you have an idea how much research is needed and into what aspects of your subject. Your next step is to get on with the research. Will you do this in the library or on the Internet? Or a combination of the two? The next sections have tips on how to make the most of research facilities.

Using the library

Do you know your library well? You should get to know what services are available and what research facilities are on offer.

On your first few visits to a college library this may seem daunting, but, with a little effort, you will be able to find out just what is available and to familiarize yourself with the layout and the procedures to follow. This effort at the beginning of your course will pay big dividends as you go through your studies.

First, try wandering around noting what is there. Books, of course, but there will be plenty more. Some libraries have developed an advice sheet about what they can offer but, if yours hasn't, then it will be up to you to find out so that you can make the most of your library. The range of products and services may well include reference books, academic journals and research papers, computer equipment, photocopying facilities, binding and laminating machines (useful when you're putting a report or important assignment together), video or DVD players, audio- and videotapes, CDs and DVDs. During your wander around the library, you should also notice rules about how the loan system works (how many items can you take out at once, is there a charge for reservations, how long do books usually take to come if they are requested from the store, do you have to renew in person or can you do it by telephone or on the Internet?), joining instructions, opening times and so on. Note where the reference section of the library is and also the general lending section. If you're unfamiliar with libraries generally, you will need to know that books in the reference section (where the books that are generally only consulted for specific information and therefore not needed for loans for weeks at a time – directories, encyclopaedias, etc. – are kept) cannot be taken out on loan. The general lending section, however, contains books that, if you are a member of the library, you will be able to take away to use for several weeks.

Insight

During your tour of the library make sure that you speak with a librarian. They know the library well, of course, and can give you a lot of advice and help. Many libraries will have an enquiries desk and it can be useful to make contact with someone who may be able to help you if you are stuck in the future.

Second, following your initial 'familiarization tour', you can start to get more specific. Look for things that will be of particular use to you in your course of study. This will include noting the Dewey numbers (library references by subject area) for subjects of interest to you. Of course, the main thing you will want to be able to do in the library is find relevant books quickly and easily and there are several tips and tricks to help you to become proficient at this. Mastering the library system early on in your student career is definitely working smarter and will save you time and frustration. Try the following:

▶ *Unlike fiction, non-fiction and reference books are not filed on the shelves in alphabetical order of the author's name. They are grouped together by subject area. Find your subject areas' numbers and keep a note of them.*

▶ *Learn how to use your library's computer catalogue. You can search this by various classifications and the most useful of these initially will be the keyword search. This can be a number of things. Try typing in your subject, e.g. politics or nuclear physics, and you'll be given a list of books on those subjects or try an element of your subject area, e.g. democracy or fission, and you'll get a more specific list. When you are more familiar with your course requirements you will be able to search for a particular author or book title. If you are in any doubt about how to use the system, ask for help. Most librarians are keen to help students to get the most out of the library and you will probably find, if you are using your college library, that one of the staff is an expert in your subject area and so will have an in-depth knowledge of the books and journals available that are relevant to your course.*

Insight

If you're researching for a specific assignment, try searching the catalogue using words from your assignment question. These will quickly point you in the right direction.

▶ *Explore the academic journals that are available in your library. These will often be more up to date than books, which can take quite a few months to reach the library shelves. If you are using your college library and are expected to refer to specific articles in such journals then the appropriate journals will be available in your library. They will usually be stored in binders – one for each year – and these journals are indexed so that you can find relevant articles. Most academic journals supply abstracts (short summaries) of the articles so that you can either read the abstract (which might be enough for your purposes) or find out whether you need to read the full article.*

▶ *Check out what newspapers and magazines are available. You can quickly scan the broadsheet papers for relevant articles for your studies and may find they lead you to further research for more academic articles and recently published books referred to in the newspapers.*

Having familiarized yourself with what the library contains and where it is all situated, you will now be in a position to use the library for research.

Using the Internet

The Internet is a relatively recent resource and it is enormous. A few words of warning before we look at how the Internet can help you in your studies; you must be aware that not everything that you will find on the Internet is true or even well researched. It should be treated with caution even if the website appears to be respectable or appears to have an academic base. There is no central ownership of the Internet, which is a set of networks that enables us to exchange information worldwide, and so there is no censorship or monitoring of any kind. For this reason you should always find at least two separate sources for information you find on the Internet.

The Internet is a bit like a library that is bigger than you could possibly imagine, so finding just the right piece of information when you need it can be difficult and time-consuming. Just as you had to have a familiarization tour of the real library, so you will need to become familiar with this gigantic virtual library.

The World Wide Web is part of the Internet and is where you will find the information you need – if you search carefully. Search engines (such as www.google.co.uk or www.lycos.co.uk) will help you to find appropriate websites. Choose your favourite search engine and put in a search term related to what you are looking for. This is similar to the keyword search you used when looking in the library's catalogue but you will have to choose your search term carefully and refine it if you are to be successful in your searches. Although all the major search engines will search an enormous number of pages in the World Wide Web every time you carry out a search, none of them actually encompasses all pages, so if you are unsuccessful with one engine, it can be useful to try another one.

At this point in your studies it will be helpful for you to find the websites that are of particular interest to students of your subject or that are related to topics to be covered in your course. You might even have been given a few example websites by your tutors or by other students who are 'Web savvy'. Make a note of these sites (most addresses start with 'www') as they may give you a shortcut to relevant and useful information for future assignments and research. If you are using your own computer to access the Internet (rather than using one in the library, for example), you will be able to 'bookmark' these sites using the computer's software. Even if you are able to use this facility, it is still worthwhile noting the correct website address – perhaps in a notebook you carry with you for just this purpose – so that you will be able to quote the correct source if you subsequently use information from the site in an assignment.

Insight

Remember that a lot of the material to be found on the Internet does actually belong to someone, so you should be careful not to copy directly from it in large chunks.

During your initial familiarization with the Internet, you will find it useful to 'wander around' on the Web, noting what sort of information is out there and how the various sites work. Look at the address of the site, as there are some important clues there. You may be able – from the address suffix 'uk' – to ascertain that the site is maintained in the UK or be able to assess the trustworthiness of the research on the site by the suffix 'ac'. This means that the site is an academic one – usually maintained by an academic institution – so will contain reliable information. As you read the information contained in a website page, you will notice that some words on the sites are underlined and, as you hover over these words the cursor changes to a hand. This means that this is a link to another page or site. Click there and you will be taken to this other page.

Apart from the search engines, you will also find that specialized directories will help you to find the information you want. Check with your course tutor or a librarian whether an appropriate directory exists for your particular subject area. The more academic courses and subjects that are studied at higher levels will often be well served by a directory of this type.

Insight

Take care with information you download from the Internet. Not all sources are reliable. It is always good practice to verify anything you find by checking out the source and by backing it up with another source.

Frequent use of the Internet will almost certainly mean that your efficacy improves but be aware that, unless you are very specific in your searches and have a very good idea of what you are looking for, you may well end up with far too much information – much of which will be useless. Having too much information is almost as bad as not having enough as it will be time-consuming and confusing to sift through it.

Evaluating your research

When you've gathered together all the information that you think you will need on the subject you are researching, you will need to evaluate the results. You will need to check that the information you have obtained meets a number of criteria:

- Is it fit for your purpose? *Does it answer the questions you set for yourself when you started your research? In short, did you find what you were looking for?*
- Can you use it? *Can you fully understand what the data you have collected proves? If not, maybe it does not belong in your work.*
- Does it help to prove your case? *The figures may be fascinating but, if they are not relevant to your case, they do not belong in your essay.*
- Do you know who wrote it or compiled it? *The author's credentials are important to give weight to your case.*
- When was it written? *If the information is seriously out of date it may not help your case.*

If you can follow these guidelines in evaluating your research, your work should have authority and the information you use will help you to write critically to a much higher standard.

Quick revision test

1 *Give one example of a primary resource and one of a secondary resource.*
2 *How does the reference section of a library differ from the general lending section?*
3 *What are 'Dewey' numbers?*
4 *What is an abstract of an academic article?*
5 *What suffix on a website address signifies an academic site?*

10 THINGS TO REMEMBER

1 *Primary sources of research are from the first hand. They include original letters, your own data, case studies and your own observations.*

2 *Secondary sources of research are from the second hand. They include most academic texts, books and articles and other people's data.*

3 *Always assess the question thoroughly before starting your research for an assignment.*

4 *Only do as much research as the assignment justifies – a short assignment needs only a small amount of research whereas a long dissertation will require large amounts.*

5 *Familiarize yourself with the facilities your library has on offer very early on in your course as you will usually have a lot more than just books at your disposal such as academic journals and research papers, computer equipment, photocopying facilities, binding and laminating machines, video or DVD players, audio- and videotapes, CDs and DVDs.*

6 *Get recommendations from your tutors and other students on your course as to which websites will be most useful to you.*

7 *Take care that you do not plagiarize work you find on the Internet – it all belongs to someone and there are still copyright rules to follow.*

8 *Always back up information you find on the Internet with another source – there is no guarantee that the information you find will be correct unless it is from a known, reliable source.*

9 *Try to use reliable websites as the basis of any research you do on the Internet – those ending 'ac' are usually reliable as are ones recommended by your tutors.*

10 *Always evaluate information you find on the Internet. Is it relevant? Does it add to your argument? Is it current?*

7

Improving your writing skills

In this chapter you will learn:
- *the different skills needed to accomplish various writing tasks*
- *how to plan your writing tasks*
- *ways of improving your writing.*

Why effective writing matters

Writing is a vital means of communication. Often it is the major means of proving to your tutors and examiners that you know your subject and have reached an acceptable level. If you are able to write clearly, getting your message across without confusion or doubt, then you will have a far greater chance of passing your course of study than if you are unable to write coherently even though you may know what you want to say. There used to be a trend – especially in secondary schools – towards ignoring spelling and grammatical conventions, preferring instead to ensure that thoughts are put down in writing without worrying about such things. This theory can have its uses but you can be sure that you will always get better marks for an essay or report that is well written with correct spellings and punctuation than one that is full of errors of this type. The reason for this is simple – pieces of good writing are far easier to understand. Spelling rules, grammatical conventions and punctuation have been developed simply to aid comprehension and being understood should be the first aim of any piece of writing – especially pieces done with the purpose of gaining marks to pass a course.

The type of writing that we will be dealing with in this book is, in the main, academic writing (rather than communication in business or with friends, etc.) and the purpose of this is to present arguments and ideas effectively, provide evidence for these arguments and to reach conclusions that have been justified in the preceding text. For this reason, and also the fact that writing is a one-way method of communication (there is no immediate feedback, so you must try to judge what will be the reaction of your readers and alter your approach accordingly), academic writing must be planned, with a carefully thought-out structure that will guide the reader through the text.

As with all sorts of communication, academic texts should be written to be understood – there is little point in 'blinding with science' or using incomprehensible jargon. Keep it simple, straightforward but comprehensive.

Types of writing task – and the different skills needed

The writing that you will do during your course may range from taking notes (when you will need to be brief and to the point) to writing essays or reports (when tight writing will be valued but points must be expanded) through to writing a dissertation (when a piece of work that demonstrates the depth of knowledge of your chosen subject will be essential). Let's look at the various writing tasks one by one to see the different skills that you will have to bring into play:

▶ Note taking. *We've already covered this topic in detail in Chapter 4, but the essential skill for note taking is the ability to grasp the main ideas contained in a text and get them down on to paper in as useful (and short) a form as possible.*

▶ Essays. *These will be covered in more detail in Chapter 8, but to produce a competent essay you will need to be able to research your topic, devise a plan for the content of your essay and then write clearly so that you get your points across.*

▶ Reports. *Again, these will be covered in more detail in Chapter 8. The skills required to write reports include research and, as they usually present data from your own work, the ability to present and analyse numerical data in a clear way.*

▶ Work-based assignments. *If you are following a course closely connected with your job you may have to produce pieces of writing related to what actually happens at work. You may need to include examples from your working life and to demonstrate that what you are learning is useful in how you carry out your duties. We'll look at this type of writing task in a bit more detail in Chapter 8.*

▶ Projects. *As a project is based on research, then this will be an essential skill here. A project will also need to be carefully planned and managed and then written up clearly.*

▶ Numerical data. *This topic often gives people problems but there are tricks that you can learn that will enable you to convey a lot of information using numbers. We'll go into this in more detail later in this chapter.*

▶ Dissertations. *As a dissertation is an extended piece of writing involving independent study and lots of research, one of the major skills involved is that of staying power. You will need to be able to keep your interest in the topic going for some time and to manage both your schedule and your own motivation. Organizational skills are particularly important when dealing with such a major and lengthy piece of work and your research skills will be well tested. Pulling together the final version of the dissertation will need good presentation skills.*

▶ Presentations. *Clear communication skills are essential when giving an oral presentation but to get to the stage where you are ready to give the presentation you will have to have organized what you are going to say and the order in which you are going to say it, so some of the skills you would need to be able to write a competent essay or notes are needed too. If you decide to use a computer to assist you in your presentation, you will also need some competency with a software package such as PowerPoint©.*

▶ Examinations. *In addition to the usual essay-writing skills, exams demand that you can also think, plan and write at speed (and in longhand!). Writing essays specifically in exams is covered in more detail in Chapter 11.*

Insight

Different types of writing require different styles and techniques – remember to consider what the purpose of the writing is and tailor your approach accordingly.

All these writing tasks have different purposes and therefore require different combinations of skills but they have a lot in common too. The main skills that are required for any of the writing tasks that you will have to undertake are research skills and an organized approach. You will also need to ensure that your writing can be easily understood and a major part of this requirement can be achieved by using correct punctuation and grammar and we will deal with this – something that often worries new and returning students – in the next section.

Grammar, punctuation and spelling

Following the rules of grammar, punctuation and spelling in all sorts of writing is extremely important. They make your essays, reports and projects easier to read and understand. If you make mistakes in any of these vital areas, your reader will have to pause to puzzle out what is being said:

▶ *Poor grammar will make it difficult for your reader to work out the sense of what you are trying to say.*
▶ *A comma or full stop in the wrong place will interrupt the flow of your writing.*
▶ *An incorrect spelling will distract the reader while they work out what the mistake is.*

It is not always easy to become perfect in these areas but awareness of the problems plus putting in an extra effort to check your work will help to ensure that you communicate exactly what you mean to say.

GRAMMAR

Let's look at some of the more common grammatical errors:

- ▶ Verb and subject agreement. *Mistakes in this area sound awful in conversation but are soon forgotten. If, however, you make the same mistake in writing, it will be there for all to see and your work will give a poor impression. If a verb is singular then its subject must be singular too. Or both must be plural. For instance, we say 'He [the subject] is [the verb] clever' and never 'He are clever', and 'They were late' rather than 'They was late.' Watch out for words such as 'none', 'neither' or 'either' (all of which are singular) or collective nouns such as 'the committee', 'the government' or 'the board' – all of which are also singular. We would therefore say 'The committee has already given its decision on this.' Having said this, a small number of plural words, notably 'data', have come to be treated as a singular 'group' noun and therefore are usually nowadays used with a singular verb.*
- ▶ Double negatives. *If you use two negative words in a sentence, they will not express what you meant to say, as they will cancel each other out, e.g. 'I don't know nothing.' This can be corrected by taking out one of the negatives. So either 'I don't know anything' or 'I know nothing' would make sense.*
- ▶ Using 'I' or 'me'. *The trick to deciding whether to say 'you and I' or 'you and me' is to see if you can substitute 'we' or 'us'. If 'we' makes sense, then use 'you and I'. If the sentence makes sense using 'us', then it would be correct to say 'you and me'. For instance, we would never write 'The senior lecturer invited you and I to the meeting.' Using the rule of 'we or us', it would not make sense to say 'The senior lecturer invited we to the meeting', so 'you and I' is also incorrect.*
- ▶ Split infinitives. *Infinitives are parts of verbs. For example, to go, to learn, to write. You should try not to put another word in the middle as this will result in a split infinitive. Examples*

of split infinitives include 'to boldly go' (as famously included in the opening lines of Star Trek!), 'to quickly learn' and 'to carefully write'. The way to avoid this is to change the order of the words. Say 'to go boldly', 'to learn quickly' and 'to write carefully'. This rule is being relaxed in common usage today. However, there is a school of thought that says you should at least know when you're making a mistake so that you will only make a mistake when it's acceptable.

▶ Ambiguous sentences. If what you write can mean two different things, then you are being ambiguous and that is never good in academic work. An example of this might be 'I need to leave badly.' This could mean that you need to make a poor exit or, more likely, you really need to leave. Confusion can also be caused by the careless use of pronouns. When you use a pronoun – he, she, they, etc. – it should be absolutely clear to whom you are referring. If there is any doubt, it is safer to use the person's full name.

▶ At the end of a sentence. Try, if possible, not to use a preposition (words such as of, to, for, about) at the end of a sentence. They can make your sentence sound clumsy. Examples of this type of error include 'The tutor is the one you will be reporting to.' To avoid this you could rephrase the sentence. In this case you might say 'You will be reporting to the tutor.' Often, with this type of error, you will need to use 'whom' instead of 'who'. For instance 'Who will you be reporting to?' could be replaced with 'To whom will you be reporting? Sometimes, however this cannot be avoided as the sentence may sound too pedantic – but being aware of it is important'

To check your use of grammar, do the following quick test.

Exercise

Rewrite the following sentences using correct grammar:

1 The board of governors are going to meet tomorrow.
2 The first boy was the biggest of the two.
3 He could not make no contribution to the meeting.

(Contd)

4 *You and me must attend the meeting together.*
5 *He was advised to quickly type the notes.*

Everything clear? Now check your answers:

1 *The board of governors* **is** *going to meet tomorrow. Remember a board, no matter how many members it may have, will always be singular so the verb must agree.*
2 *The first boy was the* **bigger** *of the two. Biggest would only be correct if there were more than two boys.*
3 *He could not make* **any** *contribution to the meeting, or He could* **make no** *contribution to the meeting. Both of these answers get rid of the double negative.*
4 *You and I must attend the meeting together. Use the test for 'you and I' or 'you and me' – see if you can substitute 'we' or 'us'. As 'we' makes sense in this sentence ('we must attend this meeting together' rather than 'us must attend the meeting together'), you must use 'you and I'.*
5 *He was advised* **to type the notes quickly.** *Rearrange the words to eliminate the split infinitive 'to quickly type'.*

PUNCTUATION

And now let's tackle punctuation.

Punctuation causes many problems for a lot of people but it is well worth making the effort to get it right as it will make your written communication much easier to understand. In spoken communication we pause naturally to make our meaning clear and punctuation marks such as full stops, commas and semi-colons are designed to show the reader where the pauses come. Some people use a 'pepper-pot approach' to punctuation – sprinkling commas and full stops throughout their work. This does not help to raise the standard of the work any more than missing out the punctuation altogether, so it is worth learning a few basic rules to ensure that the punctuation you use makes your work easier to understand.

Commas, semi-colons and full stops are *not interchangeable*
Each has its correct place in a sentence and can be used to create pauses of differing lengths.

▶ *Full stops come at the end of sentences and represent the longest pause. They are used to show the end of the thought contained in that sentence. The next sentence will then begin with a capital letter.*
▶ *Commas and semi-colons, by way of contrast, come in the middle of sentences and denote pauses of shorter length. Commas are used as follows:*
    1 To separate an introductory word or phrase, e.g. However, the essay was well received.
    2 To separate a phrase within a sentence, e.g. The letter, which arrived yesterday, contained details.
    3 To separate single words in a series, e.g. The file contained copies of reports, notes, essays and articles.
▶ *Semi-colons give a shorter pause than a full stop but a longer one than a comma. Use them for the following purposes:*
    1 To separate two sentences that are closely connected (in meaning). For example, 'The lecture was a long one; it covered many different subjects.' The semi-colon can be tricky in these circumstances and it is often safer to write two sentences separated by a full stop.
    2 To separate a series of phrases (instead of using commas) where there are already commas in the phrases themselves.

There are just two uses for an apostrophe
Apostrophes probably cause more problems than any other punctuation mark but they should only be used for the following two purposes:

1 To show possession. For example the apostrophe in the phrase 'the tutor's office' shows that the office belongs to the tutor. It can often be difficult to decide where to put the apostrophe, especially when a plural is involved. To help with this decision you should ask yourself who owns the object. If the answer is singular, then the apostrophe should be placed between the last letter of the singular word and the 's' that shows ownership. If the object is owned by more than one person, then the apostrophe must be placed after the 's' that denotes that it is plural. So, with only one lecturer for example, we would write 'the lecturer's books' but with several lecturers we would write 'the lecturers' books'.

2 *To show where letters are missing. E.g. 'don't' for 'do not', 'it's' for 'it is', 'can't' for 'cannot', 'we're' for 'we are'.*

Here's a quick exercise to check that you've understood how to use apostrophes correctly.

Exercise

Put apostrophes in the right places in these sentences:

1 *The girls hat was blue.*
2 *'That isnt true,' she said.*
3 *All the students bags were full of books.*
4 *The company met all its targets this year.*
5 *'Dont touch the paint! Its wet!' he shouted.*

Answers

1 *The girl's hat was blue. The hat belonged to the girl so the apostrophe signifies possession in this case. There's only one girl – it's not plural – so the apostrophe must go before the 's'.*
2 *'That isn't true,' she said. Put an apostrophe in 'isnt' to show there's a letter missing.*
3 *All the students' bags were full of books. Here we've got a possessive plural so the apostrophe must go after the 's'.*
4 *The school met all its targets this year. This is a common error – don't be tempted to put an apostrophe in 'its' unless it is used in place of 'it is'.*
5 *'Don't touch the paint! It's wet!' he shouted. There were two missing apostrophes in this question. One in 'don't' and the other in 'it's' – both to show missing letters.*

SPELLING

And finally in this section, we'll try to improve your spelling if you have problems in this area.

A lot of people lack confidence in their ability to spell. English spelling is not easy but some people find it more difficult than others and it is not possible just to 'learn a few rules' to solve the problem completely – but it can help. A complete guide to English spelling is way beyond the scope of this book, of course, but just a few tips could make a difference.

Many words just have to be learned but some difficulties can be overcome by paying attention to some rules such as:

▶ *Using 'i' before 'e' except after 'c' – when the sound is long ee. This will help you with words such as 'belief' and 'receive'.*
▶ *Adding 'ise', 'ize' or 'yse' to the end of words. Many words can be spelled using either 'ise' or 'ize' (e.g. realise or realize) but a few can be spelled using only one or the other – e.g. capsize and revise.*
▶ *Use 'c' if it's a noun and 's' if it's a verb. Some words sound the same but are spelled differently according to whether they are nouns or verbs. So, for example, use advise, practise and prophesy if you need a verb (a 'doing' word) but use advice, practice and prophecy when a noun (the name of a thing) would be correct.*

NB American English spelling has different rules, for example US texts use practise for a verb and a noun.

Check your spelling of some commonly mistaken words by completing the following quick test.

Exercise

Which is the correct spelling in each pair of words?

1 *Seperate or separate?*
2 *Desperate or desparate?*

3 *Receive or recieve?*
4 *Accommodate or acommodate?*
5 *Sincerley or sincerely?*

Answers

1 *Separate*
2 *Desperate*
3 *Receive*
4 *Accommodate*
5 *Sincerely*

If there are words that you know you are doubtful about, get into the habit of looking the word up in a dictionary. Frequent use of a dictionary can make an enormous difference to your spelling ability and will help to make your work look more competent.

With attention to detail – especially punctuation, spelling and grammar – your assignments will make a much better impression, could gain better marks and make you feel much more confident. And, of course, if you can improve the standard of your writing now, it will stand you in good stead for the rest of your life.

Insight

Correct grammar, spelling and punctuation will always make your writing more readable. Try reading a piece aloud to check it. If there are areas that you stumble over then examine them carefully as that is often a sign that something is wrong with the writing.

Organization – a beginning, a middle and an end

While all different writing tasks have different requirements because of their different purposes, they will all be improved by an organized approach. They all need to be planned before they are written and they all need a beginning, a middle and an end. It will help if you follow a logical approach to your writing tasks and get into a routine of how you tackle a writing project early on in your studies. If you develop a plan now, you will be able to follow the steps to produce work more easily for years to come. Whatever the writing task, the following four steps will help you to organize it:

1 Rewrite the question – *the aim of this is to make sure that you understand what you are being asked to do. It is vital that you keep to the subject. Do not rewrite the question so that it asks what you wish it had asked or asks something entirely different. The purpose of rewriting the question at this stage is not to invent something else but to put it into your own words and, in the process, increase your understanding and start to organize your thoughts. The main fault that tutors marking questions find is that students simply haven't answered the question. If there are any words in the question that you're not sure of, look them up in a dictionary or find them in your set books. It is impossible to write a good essay, dissertation, project or report if you are not absolutely clear what is required. You need to know where you are going and how you are going to get there. So, your first step should be to rewrite the question so that it clarifies for you exactly what you are going to do. In the process you will be analysing the question to see what is required. Let's look at an example of how you might do this:*

Original question: Argue the case against the banning of capital punishment with reference to recent legal cases.

First you could underline the crucial bits of the original question:

<u>Argue the case</u> <u>against</u> the <u>banning</u> of <u>capital punishment</u> with reference to <u>recent legal cases</u>.

Think about how you could reword these bits: 'Argue the case' refers to arguments so it could become 'What are the arguments?' And you could turn around 'against the banning of capital punishment' to the more

(Contd)

easily understood 'for retaining capital punishment'. When you read the next part 'with reference to recent legal cases' you can start to think about what recent cases involving capital punishment you have read or heard about and change this part to 'examples from recent cases'.

The final rewritten question reads:

Rewritten question: What are the arguments for retaining capital punishment? Support these arguments with examples from recent cases.

Now that you have gained an understanding of the question, you need to start to think what is needed to come up with an answer. Here are some suggestions for the sort of the questions you should be asking yourself as you analyse the question you have to answer:
- *What is the focus of the question?*
- *Why are they asking this question?*
- *What do I already know about this?*
- *What else do I need to find out?*
- *Where will I find this information?*
- *Is there some important research that I should refer to in my answer?*
- *Is this a topical issue?*
- *How many different sources of information should I use?*

Insight

At an early stage you should decide upon your approach to a question. After analysing what the question is asking, you should come to a decision about the *direction* of your answer – will there be one main argument or many? – for example. Setting your direction at this stage will make the writing easier.

2 Gather your information – *this is where you get all your ideas and information together and then try to make sense of them. Note the last question in our last list, 'How many different*

sources of information should I use?' The extent of your research will mainly depend on how many words the finished essay or report is to be. A 500-word essay on a major topic will have to be very carefully focused and will probably only need the information and ideas you already have in your head – perhaps clarified or confirmed by a quick look at your notes, whereas a 5,000-word essay or report will require some in-depth research and may involve several sources of information such as articles, books, the Internet, your notes, your course books, handouts from your tutor and so on. There will be more about researching information for a writing task in the next chapter.

3 Outline – *this is where the real planning and organization comes in. You've got a proper understanding of the question and you've gathered the necessary information so now you need to put it into an order that will produce a good piece of writing. Remember that you need a beginning, a middle and an end, so you should organize your information along those lines, ensuring that you are answering the question that was set and discarding information that does not help you to answer the question. Details of how you can use the information you have found to produce a competent essay will be given in the next chapter.*

4 Write – *this is the final stage of your writing task. Do not be tempted to start writing as soon as you see the question. That would be a disorganized – and ultimately unsuccessful – approach. Use the previous three stages of the writing process to ensure that you understand what is being asked of you, have all the necessary information to hand and have put that information into a logical order. Writing without planning is like setting off on a long car journey without a map or a plan of how you are going to get to your destination – you will get lost and waste time finding your way. It will take you much longer to reach your destination.*

The next section will give you a few ideas as to how you can improve the readability and quality of your writing – after you have done the planning!

Signposting and other ways to improve

There are plenty of easy ways to improve the 'flow' and readability
of your writing. Let's look at a few of these now:

▶ Signposting – *this can be a very effective way of letting your
reader know where you are going with your writing. It can help
them to follow the argument you are making. You know where
you are going with your essay or other written work but, unless
you use signpost words carefully, your reader may lose the thread
of your argument. If you allow your reader to get lost, you will
have squandered your chance of a good mark. There are various
words and phrases that you can use to remind your reader where
you have been and to point them in the direction of where the
argument is going. Remember that what will be obvious to you
in your argument is rarely as obvious to the reader so use a few
signposts to show them the way. Here are some examples of
words and phrases that can be used to 'signpost':*
    Now that we have ...
    Having considered X, we can now look at Y.
    In short ...
    As we have seen, ...
    Despite X, there still remains ...
    But before we can deal with X, we must first look at Y.
▶ Using link words – *these can be a bit like the signposting
words just discussed in that they can give the reader a small
clue as to where things are going in your writing. However,
they can also be used to make the connection between parts
of your argument and to make the words flow. To make your
argument more accessible, you must link the ideas and each
new paragraph together so that the reader can see how they
relate to one another. For example, you might use 'On the
other hand' when you give an opposing view. This will link
two ideas together. Here are some more ideas for linking
words that will help the flow of your writing:*
    Of course, ...
    However, ...

Conversely, ...
It is a fact that ...
At the same time, ...
Despite this, ...
But first we must ...
To be able to understand ...
Nevertheless, ...
It could also be said that ...
But we should also consider ...

Using link words and phrases well will ensure that your ideas are tied together so that the reader can see the relationship between them. It will avoid your ideas floating around in the midst of your writing without a connection to the other ideas and arguments that are there.

▶ Using paragraphs – *you should use a new paragraph for every new idea in your piece of writing. If you start a new argument, start a new paragraph. For this reason the best time to decide where new paragraphs start is during the planning stage. When you are deciding on the running order of your essay or report, you will be able to see where the new ideas and arguments are introduced and this is where new paragraphs will be started.*

It is a good idea to number them on your rough plan as you go along. It will then be a simple matter to start with 'Para 1' – your introductory paragraph – and include the ideas that you have decided go in there before you move on to 'Para 2' – your first argument in the body of your piece of work. Paragraphs are a useful tool in making a piece of writing easier to read in that each new paragraph will immediately tell your readers that a new idea is coming up. Use a new paragraph for each new theme or idea and do not allow them to be too long as paragraphs are a way of showing how the argument is developing – keep your readers in the picture.

▶ Sentence length – *this can be varied to keep the writing interesting. Generally speaking, shorter sentences are best. Long, convoluted sentences will do more to lose your reader than any other element of your writing, as it can be difficult to understand the central meaning in a sentence that tackles a variety of issues. If you split it up into two, three or even more sentences you will find that the sense will be improved. However, not all sentences should be very short. This could make the writing boring and, of course, this is another way of losing your reader. So, the best way is to vary your sentence length. Very short, punchy sentences can be used to draw attention to simple statements of fact while longer sentences can be used to explain more complicated ideas. It is therefore important that you are conscious of sentence length as different lengths have different uses and will give your writing texture and interest.*

▶ Summarizing – *this should be done at regular intervals during a long piece of work as this will help your reader to keep up with your arguments without having to look back. Of course, you may summarize your topic and the purpose of the piece of writing at the start of your essay or report and there will always be some element of summing up in the last paragraph; however, it is also useful to sum up as you go along too.*

This will keep your readers at ease in that they will know that they have understood what has gone before and are prepared for what is to come. To introduce a summary you might write 'Having looked at X and Y and found that Z is usually the case, we can now examine ...' or 'Despite the failure of X, Y is still in existence so ...' or 'To build upon our case that ...' Use these summary ideas but also think of some of your own and put one or two extra summaries in every assignment that you have to complete and you will find that your work becomes much easier to understand.

If an essay or report is well signposted, with a new paragraph for each new theme, varying sentence lengths, plenty of link words, and summaries to show the reader where they have been and where they are going, you will keep the reader's interest and get your points across much more effectively.

Having written your assignment or project, there are several checks you can carry out (apart, of course, from the essential proofreading to eliminate any typing errors and so on). Go through the text carefully looking at the overall structure and ask yourself:

▶ *Is the introduction clear? Can the reader immediately see what the theme of the piece will be?*
▶ *Is there a separate paragraph for each of the main points?*
▶ *Are these paragraphs in a logical order?*
▶ *Does it 'flow'? Signposting words can help with this.*
▶ *Have you made a convincing case? Make sure you have sufficient evidence for points you have made and for your conclusion.*
▶ *Does your conclusion draw the whole argument together succinctly and logically?*

Insight

Always proofread and also carry out a 'sense' check. Proofreading should pick out any typing or spelling errors and a check of the sense of your work will make sure that your work says what you meant it to say. Above all, check that you have answered the question.

Presenting numerical data

The last section in this chapter is slightly different in that it will not need too many words or require advanced skills in punctuation or grammar. However, it is a skill that you will often need when completing assignments. A well-thought-out and presented set of figures can improve a piece of writing. The analysis and/or presentation of numerical data will be used in most subjects – not just maths or scientific subjects. For instance, if you do a survey or questionnaire in a social sciences project you will need to present and analyse the data you collect.

Numbers, presented in the right way, can give you access to an enormous amount of information in a very short time. Of course, you will have to invest some time to learn how to interpret and present the information, but that will be well worthwhile because it will save you time in the long run. A lot of the knowledge we need to have in order to interpret numerical information is learned in everyday life. For example, most of us know that percentage is represented by the sign % or that a mile is further than a kilometre. However, unless we've had some tuition or plenty of practice, we may not be able to read and use the information contained in a table, chart or graph. This is where we need to invest some time.

Figures can add weight to many aspects of academic study. It is not sufficient to say that 'most' people are in favour of a change or that 'very few' families take holidays in a particular country. Far better to be able to present data efficiently and inform your readers that '93 per cent' of the people surveyed (and to be able to be specific about the numbers surveyed) were in favour of a specific change in society or that only 200 families took their holidays in Serbia in 2004 compared with 2 million families taking their holidays in Spain in the same period. These figures are all made up – but you get the picture.

There is a variety of ways in which numbers can be presented and, if you want to include them in an assignment, you must choose the most appropriate way. There are tables and many types of charts and graphs that all display information in different ways. The aim is to show the figures in a way that makes them clear and accessible – they must tell the story that you want them to tell. As with other study skills, choosing the right format (graph, pie chart and so on) and making informed decisions about how you show the data is something you can learn.

There are a few basic rules about using tables, charts and graphs that will help to make your data clear for your readers:

> ▶ *Don't just drop the table, etc. into your essay or project without explaining first what the data shows. Without this explanation your readers will be lost and the impact of the data will be lessened. Give a short introduction to the table or chart, giving brief details of how the data were collected and what the numbers show. Do not try to explain everything that the chart or table is there to say; simply give a short summary by way of introduction and orientation for your readers.*

- ► If you have copied the data, i.e. it is not your own original work, then you must note the source. Usually you would credit the source at the bottom of the chart with a brief note. See the example in Table 7.1 below.
- ► Give your table or chart a clear title.
- ► Use labels so that every aspect of your table or chart is clear. This includes units of measurement (do the figures represent pounds sterling, tonnes or percentages, for example?) – don't leave your readers to guess.
- ► Put the table or chart in the right place. This should be as close as possible in the text to the point that the data illustrates.

Let's look at tables first. Tables are an easy way to present numerical information in an organized and easy-to-understand format. They can be used to arrange numerical data so that it is possible to see the relationships between different parts of the information and to look up specific details. For example, in the Table 7.1 you can easily see which is the best-performing product group or which year was most profitable.

Table 7.1 Sample table showing presentation of data

Product group	SALES FIGURES – YEARS 1 TO 3 Sales (£1,000s)		
	Year 1	Year 2	Year 3
A	1,420	1,560	1,610
B	2,670	2,940	2,880
C	4,100	3,690	3,140
D	2,360	2,830	3,120
E	930	1,040	860

Source: *Succeed at Psychometric Testing – Numerical Reasoning Advanced Level*,
Hodder & Stoughton, Bernice Walmsley (2004).

Can you spot the product group with the highest sales in Year 3? In a well-presented table, information like that is easy to pick out – we can immediately see that the answer is Group C and this demonstrates the value of using tables.

Take another look at Table 7.1. Note the title, the fact that the figures represent thousands of pounds and cover the sales of five product groups over three years. From this example, you can see that tables are a good way to present numerical data in a compact, understandable and efficient way. Here are a few tips to help you to interpret and present information in this way:

▶ *Do not be tempted to skip tables when you come across them in a text. And do not rush them – give yourself time to understand them fully. With practice, you will get quicker and better at using numerical data.*

▶ *Familiarize yourself with the main idea of the table as a first priority – check out the title and also any other information in the text immediately before and after the table.*

▶ *Look next at the headings – across the top of the columns and down the side of the table.*

▶ *Make sure you've noted the scale – is the table telling you about product sales in thousands of pounds as in our example or production of tonnes of product or percentages of people in a survey?*

▶ *Then check the highs and lows. The highest figures in a column and the lowest will tell you the limits of the information. From our example table, for example, this would tell you that the most profitable product was product C in Year 1 and the least profitable was product E in Year 3. If you were a production or sales manager trying to decide which product to make more of or which to discontinue, this information would be invaluable.*

▶ *Don't forget to check when the information was gathered. If it represents the results of a survey of computer ownership ten years ago, then the figures won't tell you much about current trends in technology.*

▶ *Try summarizing in words just one aspect of the data presented. This will not only check that you have understood it but will also show you just how much information can be fitted into a small space.*

▶ *Finally, treat numerical data with a healthy degree of suspicion. Ask yourself who has presented the information and what case are they trying to put forward. Could they have presented the statistics in such a way that you are given an incorrect picture? This is not usually the case but it does no harm to ask yourself the question.*

Let's look next at some of the various types of graphs and charts you could use. They introduce a more graphic element to the presentation of data and are therefore visually stimulating and will make it easier to understand. Charts and graphs are therefore very useful in text-heavy reports, projects and dissertations as they help to break up huge chunks of text.

First up, the line diagram, shown in Figure 7.1.

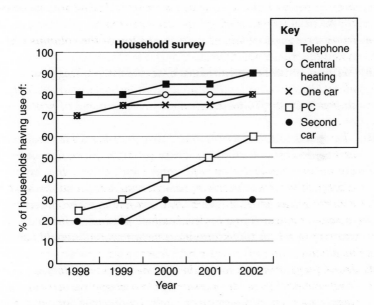

Number of households surveyed = 1,000

Figure 7.1 Sample line diagram.

Source: *Succeed at Psychometric Testing – Numerical Reasoning Advanced Level*,
Hodder & Stoughton, Bernice Walmsley (2004).

This sort of graph is an ideal choice to represent data with a limited number of categories. There are five lines (representing PCs, telephones, etc.) in this figure and this is probably the optimum number. Any more and the diagram would appear cluttered and confusing and with fewer categories, say two or three, the graph would not be as informative.

Check out the information shown in the graph. You can see the dramatic increase in ownership of PCs between 1998 and 2002 and the steadier progress of the other products. Note that the figures down the left-hand side of the graph are in percentages rather than actual numbers of households. To work out the number of households in the survey that had, for example, a second car in 1999, you would need to take into account the additional information shown below the graph – the number of households surveyed = 1,000. You could then calculate 20 per cent of 1,000 = 200 households. Taking account of each of the products and each of the years, you can see that there is an enormous amount of information incorporated in this graph and, if you add that to the ability to see trends (e.g. the rising ownership of PCs), then you will appreciate just how useful a graph can be.

Another way of displaying data is shown in Figure 7.2.

This is called a column chart because, as you can see, the various data are represented by columns. These columns can be grouped together as they are here or placed singly. With groups like those in the figure, there must be a very limited number of categories to make the information shown in this way manageable. If you used single columns, then a greater number of categories could be displayed. Look at the information shown around the outside of the figure. On the left, we are told that the cost per 100 items of each of the products is shown in pounds. Along the bottom axis, we can see that each group of columns in the chart gives information for one of five different products. On the right of the chart is a 'legend' or 'key' that tells us that each of the columns represents a different type of cost (again per 100) and how you can distinguish between the different columns. Finally, don't forget the

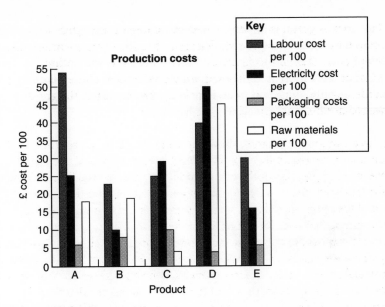

Figure 7.2 Sample column chart.

Source: *Succeed at Psychometric Testing – Numerical Reasoning Advanced Level*,
Hodder & Stoughton, Bernice Walmsley (2004).

title, at the top of the chart, which tells us quite simply that the chart tells us about 'Production costs'.

There are many variations of a column chart. The columns can be placed vertically, as they are in our example, or horizontally. The columns can be stacked rather than the categories being placed side by side. This can be useful to display proportions. In our example, with a stacked column it would have made it easier to compare the various cost components of the products. Your choice of the type of chart or graph depends on what information you want to get over to your reader. So, for example, if the proportion of costs was the most important point to get across, then you would use a stacked chart or maybe a pie chart – see the next example in this section – whereas, if the actual figures for each of the costs were the relevant bit of information to convey, then a chart like our example would be a good choice.

Finally, we'll look at Figure 7.3, which shows a very popular way of displaying numerical data – the pie chart, so called because it is made up of slices, or wedges, just like a pie!

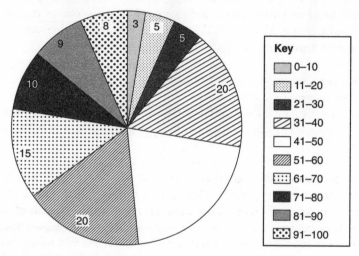

Figures around the outside of the pie chart show actual number of exam entrants.
The key shows scores achieved.

Figure 7.3 Sample pie chart.

Source: *Succeed at Psychometric Testing – Numerical Reasoning Advanced Level,*
Hodder & Stoughton, Bernice Walmsley (2004).

Our pie chart deals with a type of data that will be very close to your heart – examination results. The figures in a pie chart are displayed as part of the 360-degree whole. The figure for each category is converted to a slice of the 360 degrees that represents the correct proportion of the whole data. Pie charts are usually produced using computer packages rather than manually, as it can be difficult to work out the relative proportions of sets of data in relation to the 'pie' and therefore to be accurate about the size of the wedge.

Nevertheless, once produced, pie charts are very useful and easy to read. As a quick check on how much information you can get from a chart like this, work out how many people failed the exam if a mark of 41 or more was needed to pass. The answer is, of course, 33 and you should arrive at this figure by adding together the numbers represented by four of the wedges.

Two items are of particular note on this chart. First, that each wedge represents the actual number of exam entrants falling into that category and, second, that the key or legend on the right-hand side shows how you can distinguish each of the grouping of marks gained.

Pie charts can make a good visual impact in a report or project but take care when using them. They can be a bit simplistic and also should not be used when more than ten categories are involved as the slices become too thin to have the desired effect. It is also not easy to compare two sets of data so you should stick to using them to display proportions, for which they are ideal. Another useful way of displaying the data is to 'explode' the pie chart, i.e. separate the wedges so that you can see the distinct pieces.

A variation of the pie chart is a 'doughnut' chart – so called because it is like a pie chart but with a hole in the middle. This type of chart would be more useful to display data about a very limited number of categories as the 'doughnut' tends to look a bit messy divided into too many 'pieces' – four or five would probably be the most you would use.

Many of the tips for reading tables would also apply to reading any other sort of presentation of data (and remember that a table and a chart or graph could all be used to present exactly the same data), but there are a few extra ones that are relevant to graphs and charts:

▶ *Initially, try to ignore the different colours and all the lines and concentrate on the words around the edges.*
▶ *Make sure you understand the key or legend. This will tell you what each colour or shading pattern represents.*
▶ *Find out what the axes represent. The horizontal axis (the bottom edge, also called the X-axis) and the vertical axis (the left-hand edge, also called the Y-axis) will both have been given a scale so you should be sure to examine these in detail.*
▶ *Graphs and charts are often the best way of presenting information as they give us a pictorial representation that often makes the information easier to remember and can be used to present extensive information in a concise form.*

Choosing a method of displaying numerical data will be, to some extent, a matter of trial and error. You will need to try to visualize how the information and categories of data you want to show will look using the various types of tables, graphs and charts available to you, and you must also be very clear about the point you are trying to get across. Statistics can be manipulated to push anything to the fore, so make sure that your tables, charts and graphs present your information fairly but with the 'slant' or focus you require.

If you are proficient with the spreadsheet function on your computer, you will find that producing charts and graphs will be a relatively quick and simple matter so that you can easily see which type best makes your case. You will also need to take into account the type of document you are considering putting the information into and the audience at which it is aimed.

Insight

Choose the type of graph you use, plus the scale applied, very carefully. Simply changing the scale used can make information look very different.

Quick revision test

1 Why have spelling rules, grammatical conventions and punctuation been developed?
2 Why is use of a double negative considered incorrect?
3 Give the two uses of an apostrophe.
4 Name the four steps of an organized approach to writing tasks.
5 Would a line diagram be more effective to display data with a small or a large number of categories?

10 THINGS TO REMEMBER

1 You need to take a different approach according to the writing task as different styles of writing require different skills whether they include research skills, organizational ability, thinking, writing and planning at speed (for exams), motivational skills (especially for dissertations and other lengthy projects), clear presentation or the ability to grasp ideas and get them down on paper (for note taking).

2 Correct grammar will help you get your meaning across clearly. Avoid common grammatical errors such as verb and subject disagreement, double negatives, using 'I' or 'me' inappropriately, split infinitives and ambiguity.

3 Punctuation errors will detract from your writing and slow down the reader, so use punctuation correctly.

4 Spelling mistakes attract the eye of the reader and will make your writing seem 'shoddy' or untrustworthy. Remember a few spelling rules – 'i' before 'e' except after 'c'; where you should use 'ise', 'ize' or 'yse' at the end of words; and the use of 'c' or 's' in similar sounding words with different meanings ('c' for a noun and 's' if it's a verb).

5 All types of writing can be improved through good organization.

6 All academic writing needs a beginning, a middle and an end.

7 Using signposts, link words, paragraphs, varying sentence lengths and summarizing at intervals in your writing will make it easier to read.

8 Numbers, presented correctly, can display an enormous amount of information in a relatively small amount of space.

9 *When using numerical data in a table, be sure to explain briefly what the figures show.*

10 *Take care when choosing a type of chart – the right one will illustrate your point perfectly while the wrong choice will not.*

8

Writing essays and reports

In this chapter you will learn:
- *the difference between the various types of assignment*
- *how to plan your writing tasks*
- *how to get on with the writing.*

What is an essay?

Most students will have to produce an essay at some point in their studies as it is a way of demonstrating that they have understood, and can use, the information that they have been trying to absorb as part of their course. You can read any number of set books or recommended articles, spend hours researching in the college library and make notes on every lecture you attend but, until you have attempted to convey some of that information to your tutor or examiners, you will not have proved that you have learned anything at all. Submitting an essay will give you that proof.

So what is an essay? It is a short piece of writing on a particular topic that usually takes the form of an argument leading from a question asked at the beginning (this question can take the form of a statement or title that can then be argued with), going through the evidence in the main body of the essay and leading to a conclusion at the end.

Although an essay's main purposes are to display knowledge and to put forward arguments, it is also a useful learning tool in itself. The work that you have to do to write an essay – thinking about the topic, understanding the question, researching the subject, organizing the material into a coherent argument, planning the writing, drawing conclusions and then writing up the material – means that you will end up with a far deeper understanding of the topic of the essay than you would if you had merely read about it. While you are writing your essay it is also worthwhile thinking about how this can help with your exam preparation. Keep your planning notes – the outline and so on – as these may help you see how you arrived at the structure of a successful essay (or, alternatively, if your essay receives a poor mark, will help you to see what went wrong and show you how you can improve in the future) and will be useful during your revision period.

A good essay, like any other type of academic writing, will be well planned and will 'flow' so that the reader finds the argument easy to understand and to follow as it is developed in the body of the essay. There will be a clear introduction at the start of the essay, setting out what the writer intends to do (what the essay is about, its title, the main points to be covered and so on) and will end with a summary and a well-reasoned, intelligible conclusion at the end. It is useful to recall the old description of an effective essay:

▶ *Tell 'em what you're going to tell 'em (this is your 'beginning' or introduction).*
▶ *Tell 'em (this is the 'middle' or body of your essay).*
▶ *Tell 'em what you've told 'em (this is your 'end' or conclusion).*

Although this simplifies effective structure perhaps a bit too much, it still gives a broad outline for an essay. We'll look in more detail at essay planning later in this chapter.

Writing reports

Reports differ from essays in that they are a far more structured form of communication. Whereas essays are almost exclusively used for academic purposes, reports are often used in business and the world of work. Reports are therefore thought to be more related to 'real life' and they are likely to contain more numerical data presented in tables, charts and graphs than an average essay. However, there are some similarities between an essay and a report – they both require careful planning and research.

Many courses – both academic and work based – will require the production of reports. Where a report is a work-based assignment on a professional development course, for example, it will usually be very closely linked to the student's working life. The student may be required, for instance, to investigate a possible cost-saving measure that could be taken in their department and then to produce a report about it, evaluating the viability of the measure and making recommendations as to how to proceed. These assignments are therefore not just academic exercises but have a real purpose and relation to real life.

The accepted format for a report to be used for either business or academic purposes is as follows:

▶ Contents page. *This simply lists all the elements that are included in the report and their page numbers. A contents page would be included in all reports apart from very short ones.*
▶ A summary. *As you would expect, the summary at the beginning of a report sums up the contents of the report including the conclusions and recommendations – its purpose is to make it easy for the reader, in a work situation, to find out quickly and easily what the report is about.*
▶ Introduction. *The first two sections are then followed by a brief introduction of the report's purpose and why it is being written. The purpose here is to outline the key issues that are dealt with in the report.*

- Research methodology. *This is where the report details how the information contained in it has been obtained. You will need to describe how you have conducted your investigation, what sort of information you have used and how you have collected it.*
- Findings. *This is where you will develop the main body of your report. This part of the report will be divided into several sections. You will include the results of your research and will develop the case that the report puts forward. You can display the data you have gathered in tables, graphs and charts according to the method that will get your point across to best effect. When using data in this way, ensure that it is neatly presented, properly labelled and that sources are clearly shown. You will usually intersperse this numerical data with descriptive writing to explain what the tables and charts show and to lead the reader towards your conclusion. It is important that you follow a logical order and include sufficient detail to justify the conclusions and recommendations that will follow.*
- Conclusions. *Here you will give your verdict on the data you have gathered. You must link this in to the introductory section and show exactly how what you have found proves your case.*
- Recommendations. *Here you will draw all the threads together to make viable recommendations as to action to be taken to solve the problem set in the introduction. Always try to show the effect of your recommendations. For example, if following your recommendations would reduce costs then say so and quantify this as far as possible.*
- Appendices. *This is where you will put all the very detailed information that you have gathered to back up your case. For example, you may have taken a few relevant figures from a very detailed survey and used them in a different format to explain your case in the findings section and then this is where you can include the longer version of the data. Or you may have conducted a survey and this is where you can include a full copy of the survey questions. While the appendices will usually contain many data, you should select important numerical information to include at the correct point in the*

findings section to help your readers to understand the points you are making rather than relying on them to search for them in the appendices and interpret them for themselves.

▶ Bibliography. *All the sources you have used should be detailed here. Include all books, articles and other research.*

Insight

It is a good idea to examine as many reports as you can. Look for the different elements in the structure and evaluate each report's effectiveness. If you can identify a really good report, it will help you to see what you should be aiming for when you write one yourself.

Presentations and other types of assignment

PRESENTATIONS

Making a verbal presentation can be a daunting task. Apart from wondering about the content of the presentation, most people will feel nervous and self-conscious about delivering the presentation. But planning and preparation will help to make delivering a verbal presentation a satisfying and successful experience. Not only will good organization result in a more competent presentation but the preparation will increase your confidence and will in turn help to reduce the anxiety you may feel. As always, there are a number of steps you should follow:

▶ Set aims and objectives – *what do you want your presentation to achieve? What information or arguments do you want to put across? You might simply want to impart information or your objective might be more ambitious – to change attitudes, for example. Decide on your goals before you start and also decide how you will know whether you have been successful or not. You could give out a feedback sheet after your presentation to check your audience's response so that you can monitor your goals.*

▶ Take care not to try to include absolutely everything you know on the topic in your presentation. *If you have more detail than you can easily present, then make a simple case, including a few relevant figures and then include the unabridged data in a handout. You should aim at being easy to understand, straightforward and developing a strong case.*

▶ Check out your audience. *You must consider your target audience and tailor the way in which you present your facts and information. Take into account the age range, how formal they will expect you to be, their current level of knowledge of the subject of your presentation and their possible attitudes. For example, you will need to adjust your presentation content and delivery style accordingly if your audience is made up of people well qualified in your subject or if they are newcomers.*

▶ Plan the presentation with a beginning, a middle and an end – *as always the structure of your work is of paramount importance. Ensure you have an introduction that clearly sets out your case and tells your audience exactly what you are trying to do. Then go on to develop your points one by one – perhaps with a slide or other visual aid for each point you are making. Finish with a well-thought-out conclusion. At this point don't be worried if you think you are repeating yourself. Your conclusion should link back to your introduction and also tie in all the points you have made in the main body of your presentation.*

▶ As with written work, you should make life easier for your audience by using signposts. *In your introduction, you should let them know where you intend the presentation to lead and then, along the way, sum up where you've been and make it clear where you are going next. Check out the chapter on improving your writing skills if you are in any doubt as to how to do this.*

▶ Include handouts and visual aids – *these will help your audience to understand the information you are presenting. Think carefully about when you hand out your written information. There is a case for keeping the handouts to yourself until the end of the presentation as it can be distracting to have people flicking through sheets of* paper while you are trying to present. Visual aids such as slides or a PowerPoint© presentation should be carefully designed to enhance the information you are including in your presentation. It will usually summarize the points you are making and you can then develop them in your verbal presentation. Whichever type of visual aid you are using, it's best to reveal the points one by one as you get to them rather than having the audience read them all instead of listening to you. You will find more help on using visual aids in the next section.

▶ Rehearse – *this is when you will be able to get your timing right. You will be able to reduce or expand your material at this stage to ensure that your presentation is the required length (but don't forget to allow a little time for questions at the end). Take particular note at the rehearsal of any annoying little habits you may have that are creeping into your presentation. Things such as jiggling coins in your pocket or tapping your pen on the table will distract and irritate your audience and will not add anything to your presentation. Lots of 'erms' and 'aahs' will have a similar effect. Try not to read all of your presentation. You will have written out your presentation in its entirety and will almost certainly have to have some notes to prompt you, but do try not to simply read them out. This results in a very dry, boring presentation – and that is not what you are aiming for.*

Insight

If, despite plenty of rehearsals, you still feel extremely nervous about giving a presentation, take a deep breath and remember 'the only way to conquer fear is to get on with whatever you're afraid of'. When you get on with your presentation you will no longer fear it.

▶ Double-check everything – *make sure that your equipment works, that you've got a plug point nearby, take a spare bulb with you if you're using a projector and also a hard copy of your presentation even if you're using a computer and so on. If something goes wrong, you want to be able to cope and*

give a competent presentation rather than letting just one
problem ruin things for you. Check that the venue is set up
as you require. This means checking the number of seats laid
out and also that everyone will be able to see you. Actually
go and see where your audience will sit and see whether the
layout is right. There are lots of things that can be wrong and
the moment your audience is coming into the room is not the
time to find out that you don't have enough chairs for them or
that the plug point is too far from where you were planning to
place your computer.

▶ Go for it! – *dress appropriately (you should feel comfortable*
but, above all, smart and suitably dressed for the occasion),
stand up straight, face your audience, speak clearly so that
everyone can hear you (you should have sorted out the
pitch of your voice at rehearsals) and smile. Show plenty of
enthusiasm for your subject – that always goes down well
and, as they say, it is catching. With plenty of practice and
knowledge of your subject, you should feel confident and
comfortable so that you can enjoy the experience.

▶ Decide when you will deal with questions. *Unless you are*
very confident and/or experienced, you should probably opt
to ask your audience to save their questions until the end of
your presentation. It is not really possible to predict what
questions you will be asked but knowing your subject is your
best preparation. If you are asked a question to which you
do not know the answer, then say so and offer to find out the
answer. Try not to let one member of your audience dominate
the question period – move on.

Insight

If you're using cue cards or notes for a presentation, be sure
to number them – if they get out of order and you can't sort
them easily, it will ruin your presentation.

Tips for using visual aids for a presentation

For a presentation to look polished and professional, it is usually
necessary to use visual aids. This may include a computer linked to
a screen, using a PowerPoint© presentation, an overhead projector

and transparencies, flip charts, slides, videos, objects related to the subject of the presentation or even music. It has been proved that people remember far more information (approximately three times as much) when they can both see and hear the information than when they are merely listening. Used in the right way and at the right time, visual aids can help to make sense of difficult concepts and can reinforce ideas.

Laptop presentations are particularly popular and, if you are confident of your ability to use the equipment, they can be very effective. However, a common equipment malfunction is that the remote control for changing the slides has a slight delay and it can be difficult to recover composure after making a mess of the slide changes. You will need to decide on an overall theme (including colours and fonts to be used) for the appearance of your slides so that your presentation will have a pleasing, uniform look. However, make sure that your theme does not use too many colours. You want to end up with an easily visible, unfussy image on the screen. When you're putting your presentation together limit yourself to just one main point per slide and use charts and graphs to demonstrate points and to present statistical information. They will be far easier to understand than using figures in tables. Finally, don't forget that you can – and should – print out your notes from the PowerPoint© presentation for use during the session.

Flip charts are readily available but, despite their apparent simplicity, it can be daunting to write on a flipchart in front of a roomful of delegates. Getting the size of your writing just right, keeping it straight rather than writing diagonally across the page, and making sure that everyone can read what you have written – even at the back of the room – can be surprisingly difficult. So, unless you are very confident, practise a lot beforehand or prepare written sheets for the flip chart in advance. If you know in advance what points you want to make (you do, don't you?) and also how you want to illustrate them, then pre-prepared flip charts will save you time, potential pitfalls and possible embarrassment during your presentation. Use letters at least 2.5 cm (1 in.) high to make them possible to read. Obviously, the further away the delegates are from the chart, the bigger the writing needs to be. A last piece of advice for using flip charts – try not to turn your back on the delegates for too long while you are writing.

Overhead projectors (OHPs) are still popular and produce a large, clear image without the need for putting out the lights in the room. During your rehearsal, position the OHP carefully so that it does not obscure the delegates' view of you. Keep your audience's attention by displaying the transparencies only when you want them to be the focus of attention. When you've dealt with the topic on a transparency, take it away and move on. Leaving it displayed will distract your audience.

Professionally made videos or DVD presentations can be extremely effective but they must, of course, be genuinely relevant to your presentation and not be too long. It might be that you will not be able to use a video or DVD in your presentation as it will not be considered your own work so check this before you make this part of your plans. Used correctly, a video can break up a long presentation and provide light relief for both the presenter and the delegates while imparting useful knowledge and illustrating points you have made.

Physical objects – again, so long as they are relevant to your presentation – can be a very useful and effective way of getting an idea across and can also brighten up a dull presentation. It can give a feeling of reality to an abstract idea.

Presentations can be a time-consuming and daunting type of assignment but they are also an ideal way to learn a number of skills that will be invaluable during your career. The following skills and aptitudes will all be involved in a presentation:

- *oral communication*
- *adapting communication styles*
- *public speaking*
- *planning*
- *use of visual aids*

- *influencing your audience's behaviour*
- *control of an audience*
- *non-verbal communication*
- *increasing confidence and self-esteem*
- *timing and time management*
- *research*
- *goal setting*
- *dealing with questions and interruptions*
- *personal effectiveness.*

Use the power of positive thinking (say to yourself 'I am well prepared and competent') to get through a presentation and you will be able to look back on the experience as rewarding and ultimately valuable in career terms. Don't forget to add details of a presentation to your CV.

WORK-BASED ASSIGNMENTS

Many courses are closely linked to specific professions and occupations and will often be studied at the same time as working full time. The main reason for studying this type of course is to improve employment prospects. National Vocational Qualifications (NVQs) are an example of this type of qualification but there are also examples to be found in the wide variety of management courses studied at local colleges or independently by distance learning, and in the professions such as accountancy and nursing.

Although much of the advice that applies to writing essays also applies to writing work-based assignments – planning, structure, research and so on – there are particular things to take note of when tackling a work-based assignment. First, these assignments are often shorter than the average essay (although they may consist of several distinct parts so the total word count and effort required will be similar), so keeping explanations concise and to the point is especially important. Second, these assignments usually require you to base them on examples taken from your workplace. This means that you must choose your examples carefully to ensure success, and also to make the assignment easier to write. This is similar to the need to make sure that you answer the question when writing an essay. The example you select must allow you to demonstrate your understanding of the principles involved. Let's look at part of an assignment of this type to see the possible pitfalls:

> *Question: Describe a significant change that has recently been carried out in your workplace and explain how it has affected you and the people you work with. Identify two barriers to change and two forces for change that existed in this situation.*

The most difficult part of this will be choosing the *example of change* to discuss in your answer. Read the question carefully – it specifies a significant change, so a minor change such as someone leaving and being replaced would probably not be a good example to choose. A major reorganization of the department, a change in working practices or a programme of redundancies would be more appropriate examples. You are also asked to explain how the change affected you and your colleagues, so choosing a major change that only affected another department would not be right.

Your next step should be to identify the *principles* you are learning about on your course that are the subject of the question. In our example, you would need to bring in something about managing change, so you would look through your notes for relevant topics. When you've found them you need to work out how you can apply these general principles to the specific example you have chosen. If you really cannot see how this would be possible, then perhaps you have not chosen an appropriate example.

Another thing to be aware of with assignments of this type is that the *word count* is often very restricted. You would therefore have to be extra careful about making your answer concise and may want to consider using tables to bring in principles such as, in this example, *barriers to change*, as this is an economical way to give a large amount of information. You could use a table that lists barriers to and forces for change and then, following the table, identify which of these were present in the chosen work situation.

Courses that you could take that are closely connected to work situations and will have assignments that require you to produce writing that deals with real-life examples rather than the more academic essay questions include:

- *Professional nursing exams – you may have to produce a care management programme.*
- *Certificate of Professional Competence – a qualification in the transport industry that tests your knowledge of vehicles and regulations.*
- *Taxation exams – where you may have to work through actual examples of tax returns.*
- *Accountancy qualifications – you may have to develop balance sheets and profit and loss accounts for actual companies and to explain some of the anomalies found.*
- *NVQ in Healthcare – you will have to develop case studies based on real-life examples of the care people in your work environment need.*

DISSERTATIONS

Dissertations are quite a common type of assignment in higher education. They are a type of research project and will often be quite lengthy pieces of work culminating in a report-style document and sometimes a presentation too, so look back at some of the tips for those types of work as well as these specifically about dissertations.

If you have to do a dissertation as part of your course, you will usually find that you have a lot of freedom about how you tackle it and about your choice of topic. It will not be directed by your tutors in the same way as, say, an essay would be. This lack of guidance and focus can make dissertations quite daunting. You will have to manage the project yourself so there are additional skills to be learned. You will have to carry out extensive research, decide for yourself the questions to be answered and decide on the appropriate research sources without too much guidance from your tutors. To do this successfully you will have to develop a high level of personal commitment to the project and to manage your time very carefully. There are a number of strategies that can help you with this type of independent work:

- ▶ Start early. *There is a lot of work involved in a dissertation so it is especially important that you do not leave things until the last minute.*
- ▶ Choose a topic carefully. *It must really appeal to you and also must have plenty of scope for research. Don't choose something that you think will impress the assessors but will bore you rigid within days or that you will be unable to find much research material about. Try brainstorming a few subjects that would interest you and then check out the resources in your library and on the Internet. Finding that there has been extensive research in the area you are considering is vital but you should also be trying to give the topic your own individual twist.*
  Perhaps you will be able to apply the central question to your local area or to a group of people that you have knowledge of and personalize the research in this way. Topic choice for a major project or dissertation is particularly important in that you only get one chance – unlike in exams where there is a number of questions for you to prove yourself, you can only display your knowledge and research capabilities on one major project. Spending some time looking carefully at possible subjects at this early stage will save time later, as it will ensure that your choice is right for you and will help you to avoid a false start or, worse still, the pain of having to carry on with a project that is not right for you.
- ▶ Plan every step of the way. *With a lengthy piece of work like a dissertation, it is doubly important that you carefully schedule your time. Consider all the small steps that will lead you to a successful dissertation, list them and then make a detailed schedule of exactly how long each will take and when you plan to do them. Although dissertations are essentially pieces of work that you are required to carry out independently, you will still get guidelines from your tutors as to the approximate number of words required, how they expect it to be presented*

and when, and some pointers as to source materials. Use all the information they are able to give you to ensure that your plan is as comprehensive as possible.

▶ Keep in touch with your tutors. *If you have regular meetings scheduled, make sure that you are punctual and well prepared for them. At different stages of the project they will be able to give you valuable advice and help. They will be unlikely to tell you directly what you should be doing and when, but they will certainly be able to point you in the right direction for appropriate source materials and to let you know if the scope of your dissertation is right. They will let you know if you have chosen a topic that is too wide or too ambitious or, just as importantly, a topic that is not big enough. A good dissertation topic will be challenging but not overwhelming.*

▶ Collect sufficient data. *You will need enough to get reliable results and to enable you to make a convincing case. However, it is not helpful to collect too much information because then you will have difficulty presenting it and, of course, data is time-consuming to collect. Look for trends in the data you have collected – you can then draw conclusions from it that will add to your case. See the following section on designing questionnaires that will help you to collect data.*

▶ Keep motivated. *A long piece of work like this will demand a lot of you and you must keep your focus on the end result. Use any trick in the book to keep your motivation high – such as ticking off items on your schedule as soon as you have completed them or rewarding yourself when you reach each milestone.*

▶ Summarize your research. *Use different ways of presenting your data – tables, graphs and different types of chart so that not only do you make the dissertation appear more interesting but you can also compare the different methods and the effect they have on your data. Do not be tempted to draw any conclusions that you are unable to support with competently gathered data.*

▶ Present impeccably. *Make sure that you have checked and double-checked your dissertation, including all the data presented, and that it is bound and presented so that it gives the impression of being an important document – which, if course, it is!*

Insight

The most important aspects of producing a competent dissertation are planning and timing. If you start early enough, plan your time carefully and work steadily in an organized way – you will end up with a dissertation that does you credit.

QUESTIONNAIRES AND SURVEYS

Questionnaires and surveys can help you to find effective data for use in reports or dissertations, but the questions you use will have to be carefully written if they are to result in easy-to-use data that will prove your case.

In designing a questionnaire you should aim at a small number of well-worded questions that you can put to a large number of people. Take note of the following to make sure that you get questions that will produce answers that you can use effectively:

▶ *Keep the questions short and easy to understand.*
▶ *Make sure ambiguity doesn't creep into your questions. If the questions can be taken in any other way than how you intended them – rewrite them.*
▶ *Only a few questions should be necessary.*
▶ *Make sure that the responses you get will be clear – yes/no answers are best but make sure you can obtain, and count, clear responses.*
▶ *Check out the questions on a test group first – this can be a few friends and family – to make sure there is no ambiguity.*
▶ *Do not ask leading questions simply to get the responses you want. That will downgrade your research.*
▶ *Keep the time it takes to complete the questionnaire as short as possible while still obtaining meaningful data.*
▶ *Make sure that the responses are easy to record and to analyse.*
▶ *Keep accurate records and organize your results into tables.*
▶ *Compare your own findings with current research literature.*
▶ *Look for patterns and trends when you analyse the data so that you can draw meaningful conclusions.*

GROUP WORK

From time to time you may be required to work as part of a group and to submit work done as a group that will count towards your final result for the course or year. Group work is often used on courses, as it mimics a real-life work situation where people almost always work as part of a team. Of course, working as part of a group can be very different to working alone as the various personalities and requirements of the team's members affect how the work is done. Some members will work slowly and methodically while others will want to work more quickly. Some may be perceived as 'not pulling their weight'. Frustration can sometimes build up and the end result – a report or other piece of work – may be less effective as a result.

As working in groups can be an important feature of college life and is almost inevitably something that you will have to master in a work situation outside college, it is well worth understanding how groups work and how you can use them to their best advantage.

Let's look first at some of the advantages of working as a group. A major plus of being part of a group working on any large project is that you will get support from fellow team members. Being a student can be a lonely and uncertain occupation so working closely with others can provide support, reinforcement, social contact and a feeling of camaraderie – 'we're all in the same boat'. In addition, the large volume of work will, of course, be shared and ideas and skills from a variety of people will be brought to bear on the project, making it, in theory, easier to complete.

There are also, however, disadvantages to group working. These include differences of opinion and personality clashes that may arise among the members.

A number of skills can be gained as a result of working in groups and many of these are highly valued by employers so they are well worth working on. These include:

- ▶ *Using resources effectively.*
- ▶ *Listening to others and taking their views into account.*

- *Being able to convey information to others and, in turn, to gain information from them.*
- *The ability to evaluate ideas and to weigh up all the possible options that may be on offer in a group situation.*
- *Being aware of how your behaviour can affect others.*
- *Offering constructive criticism to others and accepting it from others in the group.*
- *Inclusive behaviour – being able to ensure that everyone is included in discussions.*
- *Taking on a variety of roles.*
- *Working with others to reach decisions or solve problems.*

Now we can consider the four main roles that will almost always be present in group-working situations:

- *A coordinator – the person who takes on this role will bring together the efforts of the group.*
- *An ideas person – this team member will generate ideas and new ways of working.*
- *An information person – this person might be the best researcher in the group and will provide data and other information to help with the task.*
- *An evaluator – this team member will evaluate the information obtained by the group and will often monitor the progress being made towards the group's objectives.*

Note that each of these roles could be carried out by more than one person within a large team.

Although there are disadvantages to working on a project in a group, these can usually be overcome if a few simple rules are followed that will ease the way around personality clashes and problems of communication:

- *Clarify goals right at the start and agree who will do what – and how success will be measured.*
- *Agree that you will all express feelings freely – but with consideration for each other.*
- *All ideas must be given a fair hearing.*

- *Decisions must be taken by a consensus.*
- *Conflicts must be resolved before moving on.*
- *Criticism should be constructive and delivered one-to-one – and will be listened to.*

Being an enthusiastic and effective team member is vital if you are to get the most out of working in a group. Not only will you be making a significant contribution to the efforts of the group as a whole but you will also be paving the way for an excellent learning experience for yourself. You cannot expect to get anything out of the group if you are not prepared to put anything in – so help the group, and yourself, by making the effort to:

- Listen. *Pay attention to what others are saying and you will learn from their experience and perhaps cut down the amount of time you need to spend on your own studies.*
- Be encouraging. *By the things you say and the body language you use, you can make everyone feel appreciated and you will encourage them to add even more to the group. You can nod in agreement with someone or speak to them to show your approval of what they have said or done.*
- Do your share. *Volunteer to take on a task – and then do it. A group member who does not do what they say they will do will never be a valued or effective member of the team.*
- Move things along. *If you think things are stuck and the group is getting nowhere, try summarizing what you've achieved so far and asking for (or making) suggestions as to how you can build on this.*
- Only offer criticism if you are sure you can help someone by giving it. *Make sure it is constructive and that it is balanced by also stating what has been done correctly or what is good about someone's behaviour. Don't suggest changes that are impossible to make and, whatever you do, don't get personal.*
- Accept criticism positively. *Listen carefully and make sure that you ask questions if there is something you don't understand. Don't react immediately – take the comments away with you to reflect on later.*

Remember that every team is a mixture of every member's skills and that everyone has something to contribute. With this – and clear goals – in mind, working on a group project can be a rewarding experience.

Insight

Make sure that no individual is allowed to derail a group project. Making a few rules such as no personal criticism, taking turns to contribute, giving everyone a fair hearing and perhaps deciding in advance how to deal with problems will help group work to run more smoothly.

An important way of working with others and of improving our study skills is to form a study group. These support networks can be formal, where you meet at a certain time and place every week or month and have a formal agenda that you work through each time, or they can be informal and be almost nothing more than a group of like-minded students who keep in touch via telephone or e-mail. Here are some suggestions for study activities that such a group might get involved in and gain from:

▶ Keep in touch by telephone – *this might be informal calls when you have a problem or want the benefit of someone else's opinion on a study issue or you might want to arrange a schedule so that every Monday evening, for example, you take turns to call each member of your group (this would work only with relatively small groups, for obvious reasons). Even the occasional phone call can help to alleviate the feelings of isolation that often accompany the more independent study that is expected today, and chatting informally about your studies with someone else can often provide a solution to a particular problem.*

▶ Review activities – *you could, for example, meet in a room at the college after a particular lecture each week and review the learning outcomes of that lecture. You will often find it beneficial to hear someone else's 'take' on what has been taught, and putting your own thoughts into words will be constructive too. Try to keep this sort of support group meeting* more formal by giving each member of the group a few minutes to go through one of the main points, while others listen.

▶ Be supportive – *everyone needs support and encouragement from time to time and, if you are all doing a dissertation or difficult assignment, for example, getting together and discussing problems can be just what is needed.*

▶ Help with problems – *this can be as unstructured as simply a sympathetic ear at a difficult time. More formally, it can be an arrangement whereby each person is given a few minutes to tell the others about a current problem – for example, difficulty choosing a dissertation topic or finding arguments for an essay. The others then brainstorm a solution. Seeing how others view, and solve, the problem is informative in itself. The person with the problem must then choose their solution and talk about how they will proceed.*

▶ Share ideas – *here you might agree that you will all read different articles or texts then meet up and share your findings with the group. The discussion that takes place after you have summarized the text you have read for the group is especially useful.*

▶ Share resources – *it might not be necessary for everyone to buy a copy of a set book. If you can agree a fair schedule for use of the books the members of a group buy in this way, then it should be possible to save money but still have access to all the books you need. Another resource you can share is website addresses. If one member of the group finds a valuable new resource on the Internet, it makes sense to share it with fellow support group members.*

Analysing the task

Writing an essay or other type of assignment is about much, much more than the writing. It is about researching, planning, analysing and organizing as well as about writing down your considered thoughts so that they are clear. Long before you get to actually writing an assignment, you will need to be totally clear about what is required of you. An analysis of the task is therefore essential.

Start this analysis by dissecting the question. Try to sum it up in your own words. With a long, involved question it can be helpful to split it into its different parts and make sure that you understand these individually before you attempt to answer the whole question. You should, at this stage, make sure that you understand how the question relates to your course – why are you being asked this particular question? You should also check that you know the general requirements – how many words are required, what deadline you have to meet and the required format (if any) that you must follow. If you are in any doubt about any of this, ask for help from your tutor as soon as you can.

The majority of academic questions will follow an accepted format and will often use words such as:

▶ Discuss – *here you will be required to examine the topic in detail so that you can debate the arguments involved.*
▶ Compare and contrast – *as you can see, there are two parts to this type of question. First, you will need to find similarities and differences between the two topics in the question and, second, you will need to examine the differences and provide reasons for these differences.*
▶ Consider – *weigh up the different aspects/arguments in the question.*
▶ Criticize – *put forward your assessment of the opinion or argument involved in the question, giving evidence in support of your reasoning.*
▶ Describe – *provide a detailed account.*
▶ Assess – *weigh up the importance and value of a statement or argument.*
▶ Account for – *provide reasons with supporting evidence.*
▶ State – *give a brief account of the main points.*
▶ Interpret – *explain the meaning of a statement and provide evidence in support.*
▶ Evaluate – *examine different aspects of a statement, giving your own judgement and using evidence in support.*
▶ Examine – *investigate evidence available on a topic.*

- ▶ Differentiate – *explain the differences between two statements or aspects of a topic.*
- ▶ Relate – *demonstrate the differences and similarities of two or more aspects, showing how they are connected.*
- ▶ Justify – *substantiate conclusions or statements, providing evidence for your case and defending it against the probable main objections.*
- ▶ Distinguish between – *detail the main points of two arguments or statements, showing the differences between two things.*
- ▶ Review – *examine a topic in detail.*
- ▶ Summarize – *give a short, clear account of a topic, including just the main information.*
- ▶ Refute – *here you must argue against and disprove an argument or statement.*
- ▶ Illustrate – *give plenty of examples from different sources to explain the point made in the question.*

The key to using this list of words successfully is to read your question carefully and note what type of instruction you are being given. Each of these instructional words will require a slightly different approach to the question and you must tailor your answer accordingly.

The next stage in analysing the question is deciding what you already know about the topic. The best way to do this is to do a brainstorming exercise. Jot down the key words in the question and examine what you know about these topics in the context of the question. As ideas come to you, write them down.

Sample brainstorming exercise on an essay question

EXAMPLE

Here is an example of how this might be done using an essay question, from a politics course, of 'To what extent are there divisions within New Right ideology?':

To what <u>extent</u> are there divisions within <u>New Right ideology</u>?

[Note the underlinings – the beginning of an analysis of the question. These are the key words in the question that you should be concentrating on to start your brainstorming session.]

New Right – blend of neo-liberalism plus neo-conservatism – formed 2nd half of 20th C (reaction against Keynesian welfarist economics, a weakening of authority and start of permissiveness)

New Right economic policy – Adam Smith, Hayek, Friedman. 'Invisible hand' 'giant nervous system'

Different views on:

▶ ***The state***
  Neo-liberalism rejects government intervention e.g. Margaret Thatcher privatization. Roll back the state. Rely on market. Less government, more freedom e.g. not state religion
  but
  Neo-conservatism supports established values, hierarchy and order, state authoritarianism, powerful state, law and order e.g. prison sentencing

▶ ***Society***
  Neo-liberalism – self-interest, individuals rather than groups
  but
  Neo-conservatism – believe society is one collective organism (tradition, authority)

▶ ***Human nature***
  Neo-liberalism – rational, reasonable, self-reliant therefore less state control necessary
  but
  Neo-conservatism – individuals are frail, immoral, corrupt therefore need state authority, order, discipline

(Contd)

► **International affairs**
  Neo-liberalism – support internationalism, globalization, more power in foreign hands e.g. IMF, market forces

  but

  Neo-conservatism – value national identity and autonomy from Europe

  Above = ideological discrepancies/contradictions

As you will see from this brainstorming session on the subject of divisions within the New Right, there is sufficient material for the basis of an essay with just a bit of research (about the examples used, for instance) needed before the student is ready to tackle an outline for the essay. We'll go back to this example later in this chapter when we look at drawing up a map for writing your essay.

If you find this technique difficult to get started on and you sit with a blank sheet of paper, thinking 'I don't know much about this topic', then you need to ask yourself a few questions to get the ideas flowing. For example:

► *Where does this fit into my course? Check your course notes.*
► *Why am I being asked this particular question? What knowledge are you expected to display?*
► *What experience do I have of this subject?*
► *Do I agree with the statement, opinion or argument in the question?*
► *How would I argue against it?*
► *What evidence do I have for or against this?*

At this point, you should have sufficient understanding of the question to enable you to make a preliminary plan as to how you will tackle the question. Do you understand what you are being asked to do? Have you decided on your central theme or argument? Jot it down and keep it by you.

When you feel you've exhausted all the ideas you already have about the question, and decided on your approach to the question, you will need to decide what other information you will need to find out to enable you to write your essay. For this you will need to plan your research, so let's look at that task in the next section.

Research

When you're starting to research an answer to an assignment question, you will need to:

▶ *Decide on the case you want to make.*
▶ *Find the separate arguments that go towards making your case.*
▶ *Search for evidence – find things that other people have written that are for or against your arguments.*

If you follow these steps, when you start to research – perhaps in the library or on the Internet – you will have an idea of what you are looking for. Look at the notes you've made on what you already know on the topic and then quickly review your course notes on it. This should direct you to what extra research you need to carry out. By now you will have decided on a central argument or theme for your essay, but you will also be aware that you need some extra evidence to prove your case as well as evidence against your case so that you can present a balanced case. You are also likely to want some respected sources to quote. It can be very useful at this stage to write yourself a list of the information that you still need.

Now you can get busy with the research itself. Go to the library or on to the Internet or to the set books you have handy. It is vital that you do not get carried away while doing your research for a specific essay. You will come across lots of information that, while it may be fascinating, is not relevant to the question you are trying to answer. Keep your mind focused on the task in hand by asking yourself 'How am I going to use this information?'

> **Insight**
> When you find information that you intend to use or quote in
> your essay, make a note of the source (author, title of book
> or article, date, page number, etc.) so that you can compile
> your bibliography later.

When you've got your information down on paper in this way,
you're ready to start planning your essay. Let's look at how you
might proceed.

Drawing up a map

At this point, you will be planning how you can get from this
collection of information and ideas to a completed, coherent
essay and you will need to be selective. You cannot include
everything you know or have found out about the topic in the
question. When you have drawn up an outline that will take
you from the introduction to the conclusion via all the arguments
you have decided to include in your essay, you should be able to
see how much of the essay can be devoted to particular points
that you want to make. Your aim is a balanced, coherent essay,
so it is important that you do not write too much on one aspect
of what you know about a topic, leaving you insufficient space
to devote to other, equally important, arguments and points.
Another problem that a plan will highlight at this stage is where
you do not have enough material for the assignment. Making an
outline of your essay will ensure that you know what you are
putting where, what points you intend to make, that you have
evidence for each argument and that all the arguments can be
brought to a successful conclusion. Do not skimp on this aspect
of your preparation. The better your outline, the easier your essay
will be to write.

Your first step is to work out the order in which you will introduce
and develop your arguments. Your plan, using the example
brainstorming session as shown earlier, might follow the guidelines
as shown in the following example.

8. Writing essays and reports

To what <u>extent</u> are there divisions within <u>New Right ideology</u>?

Introduction *New Right is a blend of neo-liberalism plus neo-conservatism – formed 2nd half of 20th C as a reaction against Keynesian welfarist economics, weakening of authority and start of permissiveness in 1960s*

New Right economic policy – broad range of ideas including those of Adam Smith (18th C), Friedrich Hayek and Milton Friedman (20th C). Friedman saw economy regulated by 'invisible hand' and Hayek saw it as a 'giant nervous system'. Laissez-faire

1st argument *– The state*

Neo-liberalism rejects government intervention e.g. Margaret Thatcher privatization. Roll back the state. Rely on market. Less government, more freedom e.g. not state religion but neo-conservatism supports established values, hierarchy and order, state authoritarianism, powerful state, harsh law and order e.g. prison sentencing

2nd argument *– Society*

Neo-liberalism believes society made up of self-interested individuals rather than formation of groups but neo-conservatism believes society is one collective organism (tradition, authority)

3rd argument *– Human nature*

Neo-liberalism – rational, reasonable, self-reliant therefore less state control necessary but neo-conservatism believe individuals are frail, immoral, corrupt therefore need state authority, order, discipline

4th argument *– International affairs*

Neo-liberalism – support internationalism, globalization, more power in foreign hands e.g. IMF, market forces but neo-conservatism value national identity and autonomy from Europe

Conclusion *Examples of ideological discrepancies/contradictions given show that there are deep divisions within the New Right*

EXAMPLE

In this example, the student has assessed the results of the brainstorming session, undertaken a little extra research, and has now formed an outline – a plan – for writing the actual essay. The student has set up their views for the introduction, defining and explaining some of the key terms, and then marshalled the arguments in favour of the conclusion that there are deep divisions within the New Right.

Note that the student has numbered these arguments so that they will know what order to put them into the essay. Note also that this essay plan clearly sets out the beginning, the middle and the end. The next example shows the final essay that resulted from the brainstorming session and the outline.

Sample final essay resulting from the plan and brainstorming exercise

'To what extent are there divisions within New Right ideology?'

With the acceptance of social democracy in the UK after 1945, a set of more radical ideas was slowly developing within the Conservative ideology during the second half of the century. These were primarily a reaction against the culture of dependency that Keynesian welfarist economics encouraged (also seen as the cause of the recession of the early 1970s), the weakening of authority in society and the permissiveness of the 1960s and 1970s. This broad range of ideas was termed the 'New Right', and was an amalgamation of two key theories: neo-liberalism and neo-conservatism. There has been lengthy debate, however, over how compatible these two are with each other. In this essay I will try to support my view that there are significant divisions within New Right ideology.

Neo-liberalism is the economic policy that the New Right advocates. It is often seen as a return to the classical liberal ideology, where the economy is held to be at its healthiest when left to itself, hence a 'laissez-faire' approach. Although the original liberal theorist was Adam Smith in the 18th century, neo-liberalism was heavily influenced by 20th-century theorists Friedrich Hayek and Milton Friedman, who reiterate Smith's conception of the economy as regulated by 'an invisible hand' – Hayek likened it to a giant nervous system. Neo-liberalism completely rejects government intervention, seeing it as a threat to individual liberty, and focuses instead on fewer restrictions on business and economic development. This stance has been summarized as 'private good, public bad'. During the New Right era of Margaret Thatcher, this manifested itself in the widespread privatization of many public services, for example, British Rail services. This move was criticized by some as 'selling off the family silver', but supported by others as necessary for healthy economic competition. Neo-conservatism would suggest a very different economic policy. The importance that they place on the established values of a strong and cohesive society, hierarchy and order are directly jeopardized by the neo-liberal free market, which is dynamic and unregulated (except by the supposed 'invisible hand'). The fact that the two stances run counter to each other, even harming each other, raises questions as to how compatible economic liberalism and social conservatism are in the context of the New Right.

The goal of the New Right has often been described as having a strong but minimal state. However, neither neo-liberalism nor neo-conservatism seems to support this aim. Neo-conservatives subscribe to a form of state authoritarianism, with strong emphasis on the maintenance of authority, 'tough' law and order, and heavy-handed punishment, shown for example in the increase of prison sentence lengths in the 1980s. Neo-conservative views would, on the one hand, suggest support for a powerful and extensive state as the only method for tackling the problems of law and order, and public morality. Neo-liberalism, on the other hand, is an anti-statist doctrine. Margaret Thatcher seemed to support this doctrine through her phrase 'Roll back the state'. Neo-liberals aim to reverse the trend towards a large and powerful government that emerged in the 20th century. It is the market that is seen to be more important than the government, and individuals ideally have negative freedom, which is freedom of choice without the constraints the state might impose. Historically, for example, this would have meant absence of a state religion, allowing people free choice of faith. So, it seems that the New Right policy of 'strong but minimal' state does not cohere to either of the two stances.

(Contd)

The two also differ significantly over their view of human nature. For both of them, their policies concerning almost everything, for example, the state or the economy, originates from their view of human nature. As in classical liberalism, the foundation of neo-liberal ideology is in the belief that humans are reasonable, rational and self-reliant. This influences a number of their policies, for example, the conception that the state should allow the sensible human being to take full control of his individual private matters. According to neo-conservatives, however, humans are frail, insecure and essentially limited. This low opinion explains their view that humans should be provided with authority, discipline and order by the state. New Right campaigns such as a return to 'family values', as important in providing structure and hierarchy, have clearly been influenced by these neo-conservative tenets. Furthermore, neo-conservatives view humans as innately immoral and corrupt, resulting in the belief that delinquency illustrates corruption of the human soul rather than social injustice; therefore harsh sentencing is popular. The fact that neo-conservatives and neo-liberals disagree so widely about human nature suggests deep divisions within the New Right, considering how profoundly their attitude can affect the ideology.

On the subject of 'society', neo-liberals and neo-conservatives hold quite different opinions as well. The former hold that society is primarily atomistic: it is made up of a collection of self-interested individuals, rather than social groups (we can see how this view stems from the liberal view of human nature too). The latter refute this, claiming that society is one collective organism, held together by the bonds of tradition and authority. The New Right combines the two into what they call liberal atomism.

Neo-liberalism inherently supports the concepts of globalization and internationalism, seeing as neo-liberal priorities rest with the interests of the economy, which is not confined to national borders. The fact that globalization places large amounts of power into the hands of multinational corporation bosses means that corporations such as IMF have unprecedented power over our democratically elected British government, decreasing its importance. This seems to go against the ideology of the neo-conservatives, who value concepts such as national identity and pride highly, and generally try to maintain as much autonomy as possible from Europe. This is illustrated in the current Euro-sceptic

Conservative party stance. Neo-conservatives also try to keep immigrant levels low and oppose multiculturalism as weakening the bonds of nationhood. These opposing values must be reconciled within the term New Right.

Not all those who subscribe to New Right ideas support both neo-liberalism and neo-conservatism. However, though there have been those who reject the idea of a free market, or who disagree with conservative social theory, it is the fusion between neo-liberalism and neo-conservatism that make the New Right distinctive. I believe, nevertheless, that it does not present a fully coherent political ideology. Although the two may manage to work together in practice, as shown by both Thatcher's and Reagan's administrations, the ideological discrepancies and contradictions between neo-liberalism and neo-conservatism lead me to the conclusion that there definitely are deep divisions within the New Right.

Look carefully at the three exercises carried out with this essay question. You should be able to see a clear progression from the brainstorming session in the first example through the outline shown in the second one and culminating in the finished essay shown in the final example.

Let's look now at how you might apportion the words allowed for an essay among all the elements that you want – and need – to include. With a word limit of, say, 1,500 words, you could proceed with your plan as follows:

Introduction: *Allow about 200 words to tell your reader what the essay is about and where you are going with the topic.*
Main body: *Use approximately 1,000 words to bring in all your main points and arguments.*
Conclusion: *Use your remaining 300 words to draw your conclusion and to bring together the main points.*

The end result of making a plan along all these lines will be a well-structured essay that has a beginning, a middle and an end. As you decide where to put all the points that you want to make, you will be able to see any shortfalls in your research and any inconsistencies in your case. As you allocate an approximate number of words to each of the main sections, you will be keeping yourself on track and avoiding using up too much or too little of the word total on a specific section. Is there anything you will need to leave out? If so, what? Do you need to fill out some of your arguments with more evidence? When you're confident that you have the right amount of material and that your arguments are balanced and all are relevant, then you can start on your first draft.

As you can see, there is a lot of planning involved in writing even a straightforward essay and it is a vital part of the writing. On no account should you be tempted to just start writing without following these planning stages. That will almost always result in a poor-quality essay that could miss out vital elements or seriously under- or overrun the word limit.

Getting to the first draft stage and editing

Now, finally, we've got to the stage where you start writing the essay. At this point you're just working on the first draft. Don't worry too much about anything other than following your outline at this stage – you will be able to improve the essay in later drafts. It can be a good idea to transfer the sub-headings from your outline and use these as the basis of your essay. However, you will need to delete these headings before you finish the piece of work – essays, unlike reports and so on, do not usually include them as they interrupt the flow of the prose. You don't have to start by writing the introduction, although this can sometimes help to focus your thoughts and, as you're telling your reader where you are going with the essay, you will be reminding yourself too. You can go through the sub-headings 'filling in the gaps' until you have used up your material and made your case. You will now have the basis of an essay down on paper and will be able to refine your work.

Fine-tuning

Read through your first draft (you might find that it helps to have left it on one side for at least a few hours or even a day or two before you do this as you will come back to it with a fresher, more objective point of view) and note where there are problems. This checklist will show you what you're looking for:

▶ *Does the essay answer the question? This can't be said often enough. The most common cause of poor marks for essays is that the student didn't answer the question.*

▶ *Lack of clarity – is any of it difficult to understand or seem a bit confused?*

▶ *Flow – does each paragraph lead on in a logical order from the last one? Have you used signposts to help your reader? (See Chapter 7.)*

▶ *Order – connected information should all be together, not scattered throughout the essay.*

▶ *Paragraphs or sentences that are too long. One point per sentence (if there are two or more points, then split the sentence into two or more sentences) and one argument or topic per paragraph (again, split them up if necessary).*

▶ *Are any points made that are not backed up with evidence?*

▶ *Inconsistencies.*

▶ *Incorrect spelling, grammar and so on (see Chapter 7) – run a spellcheck but also check the spelling yourself.*

In addition to making sure that your arguments are made succinctly and are backed up by evidence, you must also have a strong beginning and a convincing end, so read through your introduction and conclusion again. Does your introduction state clearly the purpose of the essay? Does your conclusion show exactly what your judgements are and how you arrived at them? Ideally, the introduction and the conclusion should echo each other so that you tell your reader where you are going and then tell them where you have got to.

When you have read through and corrected your essay a few times (as many as necessary), your next task is to compile a bibliography or list of references.

Insight

When you think you've polished your essay as much as you can, read it out loud – you may be surprised by the mistakes you will find in this way.

Your final task is to ensure that your work is presented perfectly. This task is made easier with the use of a computer and we will look at the use of information technology in studying in the next chapter.

Quick revision test

1 List the elements of a report.
2 When is it recommended to deal with questions when you give a presentation?
3 Why would you use pre-prepared flip charts for a presentation?
4 Give two ways to keep yourself motivated during preparation of a dissertation?
5 What are the three steps to take when starting to research a topic?

10 THINGS TO REMEMBER

1 *Essays always need planning. A well-reasoned argument is an essential ingredient and this should have evidence to support it and lead to a clear conclusion.*

2 *Reports are a more structured form of communication than essays and are often used in work situations.*

3 *Planning and preparation will ensure a successful verbal presentation. They should be organized and structured, geared to your audience, and include handouts and the use of visual aids for the best affect.*

4 *Visual aids such as OHPs, flip charts, PowerPoint© presentations and videos can help to get ideas across in a presentation but they must add to the presentation rather than detract from it – they must be relevant.*

5 *Choose examples very carefully when illustrating a work-based assignment. They must demonstrate the part that general theories and principles play in the work you are doing.*

6 *Managing your time carefully is the most important aspect of producing a successful dissertation. It also helps to choose a topic with sufficient potential material and that will maintain your interest over a period of time, keep in touch with your tutors, use numerical data in a variety of ways and make sure your presentation is of a high quality.*

7 *Taking part in group work can be rewarding – but only if you are an enthusiastic and effective team member. The more you put in the more you will get out.*

8 *Always analyse the question before starting to write any sort of assignment; identify the key instructional words in the question. When you fully understand the question and have*

decided upon the approach you want to take, you can start to research material for an assignment.

9 *If you draw up a map of your answer – with an introduction, all the points and arguments you want to include and a conclusion, along with approximate word counts for each section – you will find it far easier to move from question to competent answer.*

10 *Always fine-tune and check an essay – ensure you have answered the question and have produced a clear piece of writing that flows.*

9

Using technology to learn

In this chapter you will learn:
- *how to develop your computer skills*
- *how technology can help you in your studies*
- *about uses of the Internet in studying.*

Effective computer skills

There are lots of ways in which using a computer can help you with your studies. These include:

▶ Word processing. *This is the most obvious and popular use of a personal computer as a study aid. Proficient use of a computer when writing essays, reports and dissertations can make your work look impressively competent. So long as you don't go too far with fancy fonts, different colours and complicated layouts, work that is word-processed will always make a better impression than handwritten work. Writing using a word-processing package also gives you the advantage of being able to edit without too much trouble. You can move words around, delete them and add them without all the rewriting and crossings out that come with these tasks if you are handwriting a piece of work.*

Here are some other things that a word-processing package will give you:

1 *Word count – useful when you're trying to stick to a word limit.*
2 *Spellcheck – however, always carry out your own proofreading check too.*
3 *Storage of your work – you can always reproduce it if the original gets lost.*
4 *Writing many drafts of an essay and saving them all – this avoids the rewriting that comes with handwritten drafts.*

Insight

While the spell- and grammar check functions of word-processing packages are useful, don't rely on them too much. It is likely that you will need to write longhand in exams, so you need to have handwriting, grammar and spelling skills to be successful.

▶ Handling data. *Spreadsheet and database packages allow you to manipulate large quantities of information. You can use these packages to sort information into lists or groups, to make long, involved calculations and to perform statistical analysis very quickly.*

▶ Charts. *Very professional-looking charts, tables and graphs can be produced with the help of word-processing and spreadsheet packages. Most packages offer a choice of charts or graphs that can be produced from a set of data you have typed in and give step-by-step instructions in how to create them.*

▶ Presentations. *Microsoft PowerPoint© will help you to make a slide show-style presentation with ease, bringing in information already stored on your computer and adding special effects to keep your audience's interest.*

▶ Library searches. *You will inevitably have to use a computer database in college libraries to carry out searches for the book or article that you need.*

So, in view of these important uses, it is obvious that it can be well worth investing some time in becoming proficient with a computer. Most programs include some sort of tutorial to guide you through the basics and you can quickly become confident in using a computer to help you in your studies and to make your work look more professional. There is even software designed to teach you to type. You don't have to be an expert typist to produce an impressive-looking essay on your computer (computers are far more forgiving than old-style typewriters used to be) but learning to touch-type can make life a lot easier. You don't even have to have an in-depth understanding of how the computer works – just learn enough to be able to use it. If you lack confidence and/or skills in this area, there is lots of help available. Local colleges and training providers will offer courses to suit everyone from the beginner to the advanced learner.

If you are fairly proficient at using your computer to produce essays and reports but don't really understand how things are stored on it and are therefore frequently troubled by lost files, you will find it useful to know a little about your computer's system. An easy way to understand file storage on your computer is to see it as a version of a 'real' filing system with filing cabinets, drawers and paper files. Each of these has an equivalent on your computer:

▶ *Your computer's hard disk (its main memory) is like a filing cabinet.*
▶ *Within this filing cabinet – or hard drive – are drawers. Each drawer is represented by a folder. For example, you might have a folder (or drawer) that contains everything connected with one of the subjects you're studying and another folder for a different subject.*
▶ *Within each of these folders are sub-folders that relate to the paper folders you would keep in drawers. You might have a paper folder – or sub-folder – for assignments and another for notes.*
▶ *Within the sub-folder you would then keep all the files. A file – or document – would relate to the paper files on which you've done your assignments and so on.*

Apart from acquiring the technical skills, you will have to take an organized approach to information technology if you are to use your computer successfully while you study.

And finally, just a few shortcuts and tips to help you save time:

▶ Use your mouse – *there are plenty of shortcuts you can master using your mouse. Try a single click in the left-hand margin to select a line, double-click to select a whole paragraph, or triple-click to select the entire document. Or try using your mouse to select and drag words, phrases or paragraphs instead of using the menus to cut and paste. Another shortcut is to right-click the mouse to give you a drop-down menu.*

▶ Keyboard shortcuts – *using Windows, if you want to close a program, key Alt + F4. Press F7 to perform a spellcheck and don't forget the useful keys marked 'Home' and 'End' that will help you to move easily through your document.*

▶ More keyboard shortcuts – *this time using Word. Just by pressing the Control key and another key, a number of actions can be carried out:*

   ▷ *Ctrl + C*   *copy*
   ▷ *Ctrl + X*   *cut*
   ▷ *Ctrl + V*   *paste*
   ▷ *Ctrl + N*   *create a new document*
   ▷ *Ctrl + S*   *save*
   ▷ *Ctrl + P*   *print screen*

▶ Find function – *a valuable function if you're coming back to a piece of work and want to start in a particular place. Just think of a word or two near the spot you're looking for, type them into the 'Find' function and it will take you to the place you're looking for, ready to start work again.*

▶ Find and replace – *this takes the 'Find' function a step further and is useful if you want to change something that occurs a number of times in a piece of work. For instance, you might want to change the spelling of a place name. To do this you can use the 'Find and Replace All' function and all will be replaced by the correct word – as if by magic.*

▶ Styles – *if you can master this function, you will be able to carry out a number of tasks relating to the way your work is presented. For example, you will be able to change the style of all the headings in a document with just a few clicks.*

- ▶ AutoText – *with this facility you can store frequently used text (your name and address, for instance), and insert the phrase or words into any document with just a couple of key strokes.*
- ▶ Chart wizard – *guides you through a choice of charts and graphs to present numerical data in a way that looks very impressive.*
- ▶ Table wizard – *helps to lay out your table perfectly.*
- ▶ Change case – *with this facility – available in the Format menu – you can change text that you have typed in upper case into text in lower case and vice versa. This is useful if you've been typing with the Caps Lock key on by mistake, for example.*
- ▶ Word count – *useful when you're writing an assignment to a specific length. You can check your progress as you write so that you don't write too much in any one section of your work.*

These few functions and shortcuts are well worth learning as they will save time and help to make your writing tasks and presentation of your work easier. Do not, however, spend so much time fiddling with the computer that you have no time to produce any work!

Getting organized

If you don't get organized when you're using a computer to produce essays and other written work for your course, you will soon begin to experience frustration and, if disaster happens and the computer crashes, sheer desperation if you lose valuable work that you haven't been organized enough to copy. There are therefore two ways in which you simply must get organized with your computer working:

- ▶ *Know where all your files are stored and what is in them.*
- ▶ *Keep backup copies of all your work.*

Both tasks can be achieved easily if you develop routines that will ensure you work in a way that will minimize the frustration and time wasting that can accompany a disorganized approach. The solution to this problem is quite straightforward:

▶ Create folders that will segregate your various types of files. *Maybe you will have a folder for each subject and within each of these folders you may have a sub-folder for assignments and one for notes. The way you set up your files and folders is up to you – you are the only one who can decide what will suit you and your way of working.*

▶ Name your files creatively. *Don't fall into the trap of just dating them or, even worse, numbering them – this will not give you any clue about the contents of the file and, when you're looking for an essay you've written or need a copy of some notes on a particular topic, you will probably end up opening an untold number of badly named files before you find the one you want. The file name should describe what's in the file. If it suits you, incorporate the date into the file name – just so long as it's obvious what the file contains.*

▶ Name your file as soon as you start working on it. *It is easy to become involved in your writing, forget to save your work where you can find it, and then lose it.*

▶ Keep track of the different drafts *you produce by saving each draft with a number at the end of the document title that indicates the version. For example, the first draft of this book on my computer is entitled 'TY Study Skills 1' and the next draft will be 'TY Study Skills 2'. In that way you will always know which is the latest version but can still refer back to earlier versions.*

▶ Use the headers and footers facility. *You can put the title of the document, plus the version number, in the header and your name, the date (sometimes just use the month if work on it will be spread over quite a few days or weeks) and/or the assignment number in the footer. In this way, you will have these details printed on every page of your work.*

▶ Back up your files regularly. *You should save your work (and any other files you have on your computer – household accounts, letters, etc.) to CDs, floppy disks or an external hard drive and then keep them in a safe place. Make sure that you label your disks so that you know what files are saved on them and will be able to lay your hands on them easily when needed.*

▶ After you have backed up your work, delete any files on your computer that you are not currently working on. *This will reduce the files that you have to sift through and will, if you have deleted large quantities of information (especially graphics), free up space on your computer, helping it to run faster and resulting in more time saved. Delete all old files that are out of date or no longer needed. For example, last year's assignments can be stored on a CD or floppy disk so that they are available for reference but are not taking up valuable hard disk space on your computer.*

Insight

It cannot be stated often enough – back up your work frequently. Invest in an external hard drive or use disks to keep a copy of all your work.

This brings us to the subject of computer crash problems. Having too much 'stuff' on your computer is one of the things that is likely to make your computer sluggish and, ultimately, could cause it to crash – losing your precious work and taking up time in getting it to work again. If it is running badly, it will run slowly causing frustration and wasted time. There are simple ways to clear out your computer:

▶ Remember to empty the bin. *When you delete files and put them in your recycle bin they will stay there – taking up space on your hard drive – until you empty it.*

▶ Delete 'cookies'. *If you use the Internet, you will be storing lots of temporary files that are no longer needed. These are 'cookies' that websites you have accessed will have deposited on your computer. You can delete them by opening 'Temporary Internet Files' in the Windows folder or, for Mac users, by accessing the Cache folder in the Preferences folder.*

▶ Clear out old programs. *If you've lost interest in a hobby or now have the super-duper more up-to-date version of your*

favourite game, then ditch the programs you no longer use.
Make sure that you delete the entire program rather than just
deleting the desktop shortcut or the directory for a program.

Using your computer and taking care of it in this way will help
to avoid problems and takes much less time than sorting out a
disaster caused by neglect or lack of organization.

Time management is another issue of which you should be aware
when using a computer to help you with your studies. Unless
you are exceptionally skilled at sorting out computer glitches,
crashes and problems, you should expect to have to build a bit
of time into your schedule to keep things running. As we saw
earlier, you can do some basic 'tidying up' of your hard disk
and this will help to head off some of the problems that are
sometimes caused by a computer that is running low on memory.
You will need to allow time for regular clearing out of unused
files and programs plus learning how to deal with common
problems. You will manage your time better if, when facing a
deadline for an assignment, you do not ignore the problems
that can occur.

Insight

Get to know how to escape a computer crash – the most
common way is press Ctrl, Alt, Del. If all else fails, switch
your computer off for a few seconds and then back on again.

As we saw earlier, a computer can be used for so much more than
the production of professional-looking assignments. If you have
an Internet connection (or go to the library to use their facilities),
you will be able to do a lot of your research online. You will also
be able to use electronic mail facilities to keep in touch with your
tutor and other members of your study group. In fact, if you are
studying a distance-learning course, it can be the very best way of
sending your assignments for marking, as well as sending queries
about the course material to your tutor. It is quick and easy and
will mean that you have a record of what has been sent and when.
Yet again, you will have to take an organized approach to using

your computer. E-mail software has facilities to store different types of sent or received items of mail in different folders and will date and time the transmission – in this way you can keep track of your work.

What is e-learning?

E-learning could be defined as any learning that is supported or made easier by the use of information and communications technology. It can be anything from a part of your course materials being made available to you via a computer or assignments being marked via computer right through to a whole course being provided – and assessed – online. Let's look at some of the ways that aspects of your course can be supported by electronic means:

▶ Networked information – *this is the most straightforward use of e-learning. Many colleges and university libraries have linked their computers and made available through this network CD-ROMs that contain some of the more popular and useful journals. It is often easier to access articles and information in this way than to use paper-based texts because of the extensive and rapid search facilities. You will be able not only to go straight to the relevant piece of work in a journal but also to access the same information at the same time as other students.*
▶ Other reading materials may be provided electronically – *items such as course handouts, lecture notes, up-to-date information on your course and its schedule and revision notes.*
▶ Communication – *online communication can help in all sorts of ways to support your learning. It may give you greater access to your tutors or it may foster online support groups for your course. Students can often feel isolated, but it is now possible to keep in touch online and to have access to a tremendous level of support from fellow students or your tutors. You may also have assignments delivered to you*

electronically and then be able to submit them online – saving time and paper.

▶ Online assessment – *some or all of your assignments may be assessed via computer. This might take the form of a set of multiple-choice questions for you to answer that will be automatically marked and the result – and possible comments – immediately transmitted to you so that you will be able to take remedial action if problems are uncovered.*

▶ Design software – *programs are available that will help you to design surveys or questionnaires and also to help you to analyse the data that you collect.*

▶ Interactive programs – *this type of material is becoming more common, although it is expensive to produce. With an interactive element, learning materials on computer can individualize the direction the learning takes and the speed at which it is delivered according to the responses received from each learner. This type of program can be used, for example, to develop technical skills or to take part in simulated exercises or case studies.*

▶ Complete courses – *a whole course can be studied via a computer. This may be by using a CD-ROM where the advances in technology in recent years mean that the courses and tutorials provided in this format include sophisticated graphics, interactive aspects and marking systems to give an ideal learning environment without the student having to leave their home. Or it may be by logging on to a learning provider's website. We will look at these online courses in more detail in the next section.*

With all these choices available, it would be easy to sign up for everything available online. Before you know it you could find all your time taken up chatting online, e-mailing fellow students, searching complicated databases of information and dealing with the computer problems that will inevitably occur. As with any other learning medium, you must be selective. Find the ways you can use a computer that will enhance your learning and make life easier for you.

More and more universities and colleges are embracing the technology available to help their students and are setting up virtual learning environments (VLEs). When a student logs on to the website from their home or using the college's facilities, they can work independently using the learning materials made available via the VLE. Logging on will also bring up features such as details of the individual student's progress against targets. In this way, students must take responsibility for their own progress and have all the details they need continually available. VLEs can also incorporate the following:

- *Bulletin boards.*
- *A course overview and outline – useful when trying to get to grips with what you are aiming at, as we saw in Chapter 2.*
- *Conferencing facilities.*
- *A calendar.*
- *Automatic reminders about assignment deadlines, exam dates, etc. tailored to individual students.*
- *Course materials, notes and handouts.*
- *Assessment materials.*
- *Tracking tools – to be used either by students to monitor their own targets and deadlines or by tutors to monitor levels of activity.*
- *An online chat room for students of the university as a whole or one restricted to a particular course.*

As these types of facility become more widely available, the amount of information readily obtainable by students will, of course, increase and their studies will be made easier – and hopefully more successful – as a result.

Insight

Virtual learning environments (VLEs) are helpful but care must be taken that some of the facilities such as online contact with other students and bulletin boards do not become a substitute for work. If the activities do not contribute to output, then limit the time spent on them.

Online courses

An enormous variety of courses are available to buy and complete online. They range from degree and MBA courses to practical skills courses.

The main advantage of online courses is their flexibility. As courses offered in this way can be studied in 'bite-sized chunks', they can be accessible to many more learners than conventional full-time courses. A conventional degree student would usually need to attend college or university every day and would not be able to carry out any other occupation than perhaps a part-time job. This obviously has financial implications and therefore excludes many people from further and higher education. The flexibility of online courses makes high-level courses accessible to many people – especially mature students who may have jobs and family responsibilities to consider. In addition, as online courses can be made available to a far greater audience, they become much more affordable. The materials for these courses are usually very expensive to produce but economies of scale ensure that their costs compare favourably with conventional university education.

When studying a course online, a great amount of self-discipline is necessary. If you are the sort of person who doesn't complete an assignment unless reminded several times by your tutor of the consequences of not handing it in, then using e-learning in this way is unlikely to be for you. If, on the other hand, you are a well-motivated person who has little problem in working independently, then online courses might be an ideal way to improve your qualifications. It is possible to complete these courses in your own time, fitting them in to your existing work patterns or around family commitments – and maybe a social life too. Online courses can be completed at home, in your workplace (if it is a work-based course or your employer is encouraging you to study) or in a specially established learning centre. Training providers may offer the use of these centres as well as offering a package of support and guidance.

Online debating

Online debating is part of the increase in e-moderated learning that has taken place over recent years. The moderator of the online debating forum will often ask questions to stimulate debate in appropriate areas and this can be a very worthwhile learning experience. It provides an opportunity to learn from others while organizing and expressing your own thoughts and knowledge of the subject. Debating face to face can be a daunting experience; however, if done online, the intimidation of taking part in a discussion is lessened and will lead to more participation. If this facility is offered in your college or university, it is worthwhile taking advantage as, properly moderated and targeted, online debating can reinforce learning.

Insight

Online courses are great for some students and less so for others. You need to weigh the advantages (e.g. accessibility and flexibility in when and where you complete the course) against the disadvantages (e.g. cost, isolation and the discipline needed) when deciding if it is for you.

Quick revision test

1 What shortcut would you be using if you pressed Ctrl + N?
2 What facility would you use to include the assignment number at the bottom of every page in a document?
3 How can e-learning help to overcome problems of isolation for a student?
4 What is a virtual learning environment?
5 Give one advantage and one disadvantage of an online course.

10 THINGS TO REMEMBER

1 *Becoming proficient at using a word-processing package will ensure that you are able to present your work properly.*

2 *Always back up your work to avoid losing it if you have any problems with your computer.*

3 *Don't get sidetracked on the computer; make sure you are still focusing on the work you need to do for your course.*

4 *Get organized when working on your computer by developing a system for storing electronic files such as using folders to segregate different subjects, and maintain it.*

5 *Don't let your computer get cluttered – build time into your plans to clear out the recycle bin on a regular basis, delete old e-mails or files you no longer need, clear out old programs and delete cookies.*

6 *You can also use your computer to manage data, compile charts, graphs and tables, produce presentations and for research.*

7 *Be selective about what you get involved in online. Forums, networking sites and e-mails can be time-consuming.*

8 *You can support your studies by electronic means via networked information provided by your college, online communication with your tutors or online support groups. Some assessments, or even whole courses, can also be found online.*

9 *If your college offers a virtual learning environment (a VLE), make sure that you take an organized approach to using it as you will be responsible for your own progress. Self-discipline is essential if you choose to study a course online. If you find*

it difficult to meet deadlines and need a lot of interaction with your tutors and/or other students, this may not be for you.

10 *Online debating can reinforce learning and is well worth a try, especially as it can be far less daunting than face-to-face debating.*

10

Revision skills

In this chapter you will learn:
- *about the purpose of revision*
- *how to organize your revision*
- *some revision techniques.*

Revision – not the time to learn something new

The purpose of revision is to go through materials that you have already studied, in preparation for an examination. An examination gives you the chance to pull the entire course together and to look at the bigger picture. Rather than concentrating on just one aspect, as assignments usually do, revising for exams should cover the whole of your course. Revision does not normally mean that you will be learning something new. Instead it allows you to re-examine materials and commit them to memory so that your tutors or external examiners can see that you have understood the material for your course and can use the knowledge you have gained.

There are many effective ways of revising and there are just as many ways of wasting time in the name of revision. Let's look at some of the pitfalls involved in revising for examinations:

▶ Reading through notes and other materials repeatedly. *This is not likely to be very effective (you may learn a little as a result of the repetition but not as much as you could learn by other methods) and it will be boring. Being bored while you're revising is something you should avoid, so putting a little extra effort into finding the revision techniques that are right for you will pay dividends.*

▶ Writing out essays that you've done as part of your coursework. *Although this could be viewed as active learning, this wastes time because it is highly unlikely that exactly the same question will come up in the exam. The questions you have been answering as part of your coursework have different aims from those you will encounter in the examination. You would be working far more effectively if you devised new exam-type essay questions and practised writing essays under exam conditions – more of this later in this chapter.*

▶ Thinking that you must sit for hours studying a troublesome topic. *You can learn a lot in very short – but intensive – spells, so make the most of the 10 or 15 minutes you have available before lunch, the time you spend travelling by bus, train, or while someone else is driving and while you're having a quick coffee. Be prepared for these short bursts of revision activity by always carrying some work with you.*

▶ Getting bored. *Find different techniques for your revision, use active learning techniques, shorter periods of study and more variety (perhaps switching from subject to subject) to stave off boredom.*

▶ Procrastination. *Make a timetable for your revision time and plan in all the other things that you absolutely must do so that you do not use them as an excuse not to start revising. Plan to give yourself the occasional reward too – perhaps an evening out with friends or watching a bit of television.*

▶ Extreme stress. *Remember that stress can be a positive force as it should push you into an intense period of revision. You should also acknowledge that everyone wants you to pass. There is no trickery or mystique – exams are a straightforward way of you showing the knowledge you have gained during your course.*

There are ways to avoid all of these common pitfalls and, as always, getting organized is vital. Arranging your materials before you start (but don't let this take you too long or use it as an excuse not to start the actual revision!) can help you not only to see more clearly what lies ahead but to put you in the right frame of mind. You should also plan the revision strategies you are going to use at this stage – more on these topics follows.

Making a plan

Scheduling your revision – and sticking to it as much as you possibly can – is really important. Many people wonder when they should start revising and the only answer to that is 'as soon as possible'. It is a good idea to keep revision in mind when you are first producing and collecting the course materials – right from the very beginning of your course. You can do this in a number of ways:

▶ Go quickly through your work on a regular basis. *This will not only help you to become really familiar with the material but will also allow you to see the inconsistencies and problem areas that will inevitably creep in.*

▶ Make revision cards as you go along. *When you finish studying a topic, summarize the main points on an index card and file it away – ready for revision time.*

▶ Plan your studying timetable to leave you plenty of time for revision at the end of studying new topics. *If you are the sort of person who leaves all their assignments until the last minute, you will find that this will encroach on time that could have been used for revision.*

▶ Make your notes as clear and brief as possible. *Muddled notes that ramble on without making the key points clear will be boring and time-consuming to produce and will be of little use when it comes to revision time. Produce your notes with revision in mind.*

Having said that revision should be considered – and carried out – alongside the rest of the work on your course, the reality is that many students leave serious revision almost until the last minute.

Even if you have managed to be conscious throughout the course of the forthcoming examination, you will no doubt find that your revision will become much more intense immediately before the exam. For this period you will need a plan. You will become more organized and probably much calmer if you draw up a detailed timetable covering this period of revision. There are a number of activities that you must fit into this plan:

▶ Sorting out your course materials – *see the next section.*
▶ Summarizing your notes and handouts – *this is an important revision technique. We go into more detail later in this chapter.*
▶ Looking at past examination papers – *this is an invaluable revision technique that will point you in the right direction of what to revise. More detail later in this chapter.*
▶ Practising answering exam questions – *this revision technique works on two levels: first, it gives you confidence as you become familiar with both the exam format and the subject matter of your course and, second, active revision like this will deepen your understanding of your course materials.*
▶ Normal life – *if you have a job as well as being a student, you will need to plan that into your schedule before you start to allocate time to revision. You'll also need to plan in travelling, food preparation and eating, sleep and time for family responsibilities – all the things that are necessary to keep life going.*
▶ Relaxation – *of course, examinations will be important to you but they are not life-threatening. So, treat them sensibly and allow yourself a life outside your course and exam revision. With an appropriate and moderate amount of free time planned into your schedule immediately prior to the exam, you will find that you will enter the exam room in a calmer frame of mind and will cope with the revision period much better than if you tried to spend every spare minute revising.*

You may have noticed that there are one or two activities not included in this list – trying to memorize all your course notes is not advisable, neither is spending your every waking hour frantically revising everything you can lay your hands on. An exam is *not a test of your memory*. They are not designed to see just how big a proportion of your course notes you can regurgitate. Rather you are being tested on how much of your course you have understood and can now use. Your revision plan should therefore be geared towards active revision that will help you to deepen your understanding of the work you have covered. It should not involve endless, mind-numbing rereading of your notes or set books.

Now that you have seen what should – and should not – be included in your revision timetable, you can begin to pull it together. Draw a schedule of the 168 hours in each week of your revision period. First, block out time for sleep plus work and family commitments, add in a few hours of relaxation and then you will be able to see how many hours are left that you can realistically devote to your revision activities. Before you start to add revision activities to your timetable, make sure that you have a good understanding of the proportions of your course. Reviewing the course – knowing exactly what the course has involved – will help you to see how you should be allocating your revision time.

Insight

When planning your revision timetable, make sure that you place particular emphasis on the topics that have formed the core of your course. Some areas will be more important than others and if you become very familiar with your course, you will know which are the areas on which to concentrate.

Plan to organize your notes and other materials early on in your revision schedule and then make your next task condensing all your materials to make revision easier. We'll cover this in the section on revision techniques. After these two tasks have been accomplished, you will be able to plan in all the other activities that will help you to pass the examinations. Make sure that the time you allow for each subject area is proportionate and that the revision activities you are planning in are relevant, effective and varied. If you simply plan in revision time – without specifying an activity – you may find yourself reading aimlessly and this will be a waste of your valuable time. Be more specific by planning in, for example, a period of time to condense notes on a particular topic or write a practice essay under exam conditions. Think carefully about what areas you want to revise and what activities would be appropriate to these areas and to you. You may find that you find writing essays under examination conditions very stimulating and productive but don't enjoy working on revision with other students. In this case, plan in more of what helps and less of what doesn't!

Of course, you will probably not stick to your revision schedule completely but the act of drawing it up and thinking about what works for you and what doesn't will be productive in itself. Try to keep to the schedule as far as you can, as it will keep your mind focused on the exam.

Focus is a vital asset when exams are approaching and most people who find settling down to revision difficult will lack this ability to home in on what really matters. Let's look at a typical example of an unfocused student. She knows she should revise, as the exam date is approaching fast. In fact, she meant to start a few weeks ago but she had a problem at work and then it was her boyfriend's birthday and then she was a bit short of money so she couldn't afford to buy some extra paper, index cards and files so that she could get organized. Now she's starting to panic. Getting more and more anxious as the days pass, she comes home from work one Friday evening and resolves to get down to some real work that very night – after she's watched her favourite television programme. At 9.30 p.m. she gets her books out and feels so tired that she takes nothing in before going to bed at 11. The following morning she's up bright and early and intends to spend the whole day studying. She stares at her books, thinking she should read through this passage four or five times because it's obviously very important. She's bored and her mind wanders, thinking about all the things she could be doing around the house.

She realizes she's not concentrating very well and makes herself a cup of coffee and returns to her books with new determination.

Now it's nearly lunchtime so she has a break and reconsiders her plans. All day with the books would drive her into a stupor so she goes out for a walk and spends a couple more hours with those same books when she returns. On Sunday morning, she gets up having realized overnight that she's wasted the whole of Saturday and that her real problem is not a lack of ability to study or concentrate – or even a lack of time – but that she is not organized. She has finally realized that she will get nowhere with her revision if she doesn't work out a strategy. Sitting staring at books is time-consuming and ineffective. With some clean sheets of paper, she works out how much time she can realistically spare in the next few weeks before the exam and, allowing herself some time for phoning friends or watching a bit of television, she decides on the revision techniques that will help her and assesses just what she needs to do to pass the exam. Ultimate result – success and satisfaction!

Don't be the disorganized student – make a plan. Now!

If you're still resisting making a structured plan for your revision period (maybe because you are trying to avoid working harder – after all, you already work hard enough, don't you?), then you must take on board the fact that you are not being asked to work harder but to work *smarter*. With a timetable you will not work more hours than without one (think of our student who sat for hours staring at her books but absorbing nothing, making no progress) and you will not have to perform feats of stamina or superhuman concentration. With a plan you will work at relevant tasks, for predetermined times and with your own aims and aptitudes taken into account.

Insight

Getting organized is not a matter of working harder and longer – it is a way of working smarter.

One final piece of advice about working to a timetable – be prepared to modify it. If, for example, you had planned to work on writing essays under exam conditions for two hours first thing on

Monday morning but find it difficult to concentrate and think you would be better doing a few shorter tasks to get you into the swing of things and get your brain going, then change your plan. It's your plan and it should work for you and bring you closer to your goals. So long as you're making changes that will help you to get through the revision and help you to pass the exam, then tweak the plan as much as you like.

Insight

The last item in your revision schedule – after all the examinations – should be a treat for you. Plan to reward yourself when all the revision is over with a social event or shopping trip.

Organizing notes and other materials

First, a word of warning – although getting organized is essential, do not let this task become just another way of putting off the start of your revision proper. If you let sorting out all the junk in your drawers and all the piles of notes on your desk take too long, it will be counterproductive. Plan it into the start of your revision timetable and do the minimum that is needed to get your notes and other materials into a state where you're ready to do other revision tasks.

Sorting out your course materials at this stage is part of the task of getting organized in preparation for a period of revision. Of course, it would have been better to have kept the notes and so on in an organized state throughout your course, but if you're looking an exam date in the face, then it's too late for regrets. So, how should you tackle the task of organizing notes? Your first job is to get all your piles of paperwork together. Gather up all the loose papers that are scattered on your desk, all the bulging files on your shelves, your course overview (you *did* produce an overview of your course right at the beginning of your studies, didn't you? – see Chapter 2 for more details), any past examination papers you have collected, your course books, copies of articles that you thought were essential and all the other bits and pieces that relate to your course including the loose papers in your bag or under your bed! Put like with like – i.e. everything related to each individual subject in one pile per subject and an extra pile for general items such as your course overview or exam papers. Just this small act will probably make you feel more organized.

While you're sifting through paperwork, use the time to also get a picture of what you have and how you will be able to use it to do the necessary revision. In fact, this should help you on to the path of deciding what revision you should do. Take particular note of the overview and learning outcomes for your course. These are important because they will guide you as to what you should be aiming at with your revision plan. Topics that are specifically mentioned in the learning outcomes will be likely to figure somewhere in the examination. Note the balance of different topics in each of the subject areas you are studying and be honest about how much of the course you have already mastered. If there are areas that you feel comfortable with and you are fairly confident that you will be able to answer almost any question on that topic, then you may be able to skim through those areas and spend more of your revision time on areas you are less confident about.

Having organized your materials and got a realistic view of what you need to do to pass the exam, you are now in a position to start your revision in earnest.

Revision techniques

Revision is not easy. When you see the mounds of notes and piles of books and realize that the examination is a very short time away, it can be extremely daunting. The key to keeping your interest and making the time and effort that you put into your revision worthwhile is to make sure that you use active revision methods rather than passive ones. Passive methods such as rereading your notes or copying out chunks of books or articles may be covering the right material but the chances of your retaining and understanding much of it are slim. You need to engage with the material to ensure that you are using your time to best effect. So, active methods such as condensing your notes or practising essay questions will be the more effective way to learn. In addition, using a variety of techniques will help to keep you interested in your revision and will make sure that you cover different angles too.

Remember that exams are an opportunity to display your understanding of the subjects you have studied. You should not view them as a test of memory. If you tried to memorize the whole of your course you would not only be guaranteeing boredom for the whole period of your revision but also be planning to fail. You will already, of course, have an understanding of your course materials and your revision should further that understanding. You will need to remember the basic points of any topic but, other than that, it is not your memory but your understanding that will ensure success. Try a combination of these revision techniques (they are all active methods) to improve your understanding of your course materials:

▶ Condense your notes – then condense them again. *Take a topic and aim to write everything you need to know about it on one A4 sheet of paper. Note that I did not say write everything you know – but everything you need to know. This means that as you write you should be deciding which are the most important bits of information. Write these down and discard all the extraneous detail. At this point you are trying to integrate all the different sources of information that you have collected on the topic. If you can develop a set of these sheets of paper covering your whole course, you will have a valuable asset. You could then refer to these sheets frequently in the run-up to the exams – it won't take long to read an A4 sheet of paper. But you can take this a step or two further. Take one of these sheets of important facts and condense it even more until you can get the really important information about that topic on to an index card (usually 10 × 15 cm* or 4 × 6 in.). This will take an even shorter amount of time to read and will be handy to carry about with you as you approach the exam period. You could then try to distil this information into just a few key words and phrases – maybe 10–15 – that will encapsulate the topic and act as triggers. When you recall these words under exam conditions, they will spark off your understanding and memory of sufficient detail of the whole of the topic – or at least the part of that topic that you need to use in answering the question. If you can get to the index card stage for all the major subject areas in which you are sitting exams, you will be able to carry the cards about with you in the period immediately prior to the exams and use the odd bits of time that you have (while you're waiting for a bus, having a coffee or before you go out in the mornings) to quickly run through the whole of your course. If you do this frequently, you will find that you retain most of the key points. The aim with this revision technique is not only to provide you with some quick and easy notes to revise at the last minute but also to ensure that you work actively with your materials. While you are condensing your notes, you are engaging with the material, understanding it and manipulating it. This will mean that you are far more likely to be able to use the information under exam conditions.

▶ Selecting topics to revise. Take care with this technique. Just revising the bits you've enjoyed during the course or the sections you find easy will not necessarily help you to pass the exam. You should be finding out – if you don't know already – what the most important topics are in each subject and revising these thoroughly. You will probably need to do a bit of detective work to decide what to revise. You can look at exam papers from previous years (more of this later), check your course outline and overview to see what topics are given prominence, and ask your tutors. They may be able to give you some guidance on what to revise but they may feel unable to be too specific. In any event, pay particular attention to the topics they concentrate on in the last few lectures or tutorials. Although it can help to try to reduce the amount you must revise, do not take this method too far or use it as an excuse *not to revise sufficiently. Most exams cover a representative sample of the course.*

Insight

Take great care when selecting the topics you will revise. Most courses culminate in an exam that covers most of the course and it would not be wise to ignore chunks of the course when setting out your revision plans.

▸ Use past exam papers. *These are often available in your college library or your tutors will tell you how you can obtain copies. It is useful to examine as many as possible so that you understand the type of questions that will be asked – the structure of the exam, the format of the questions, how long is allowed for each question and so on. This revision technique will ensure that you don't turn over the exam paper in the exam and get a shock, realizing that your revision has not been geared to the type of questions you see in front of you. Do some analysis of the papers by checking which questions or topics come up regularly. If a version of a particular question is asked every year, then it is obviously considered an important part of the subject and you should ensure that you are competent in answering that type of question.*

▸ Practise answering essay questions. *This technique follows on from the last one. With a good supply of past examination papers you can use the questions as practice. This will ensure that not only do you get a deeper understanding of the topics you are covering, but also you will be gaining vital practice in putting together answers to suit the exam.*

Your first task (after you have analysed the papers as just discussed) is to take note of the way the questions are worded. Look back to Chapter 8 where we discussed the key words used in essay questions. Do you need to 'compare and contrast' or to 'discuss with examples'? Work out your approach to each of the different types of question. Try to develop an essay outline for each question on all the papers you have. Brainstorming the question and producing an outline will show you how much you know – and don't know – about the topic. It will also give you valuable practice in essay planning for an examination. If you do enough of this type of revision, you are unlikely to be too worried about doing it under exam conditions.

You should then take these outlines and produce essays from some of them – as many as you have time for. Time yourself and if you have difficulty producing an essay in the time that would be allowed in the exam, ask yourself – and perhaps your tutors too – if you are writing essays that are too long or too detailed. Consider what is required by the examiners. If you have only 40 minutes to write an essay in an exam, you will not be expected to produce something that tells all you know about a topic in 5,000 words! Focus on the question – what is being asked, what part of the topic you should concentrate on, what you should leave out – and then try again.

► Practice and focus. *This will ensure that you are capable of producing competent, succinct answers under exam conditions. While you're doing this, don't forget that in the actual exam you will have to write your answers longhand. If you're used to producing all your course assignments using a computer, you may find that you need some practice now to increase your handwriting speed and legibility. It is vital that you attempt some practice at producing essays from exam questions like this so that you can iron out any problems before the day of the exam.*

► Record yourself. *If you find that you are spending a lot of time when you are unable to sit down with a pen and paper – when you are travelling, for instance – you may find it useful to record yourself reading some of your condensed notes so that you can play them over and over again. If you get distracted by things happening around you, don't worry. If you listen to the same tape enough times, you will be distracted at a different point each time and will eventually have covered the topic in its entirety. This is a good technique to allow you to use otherwise 'dead' time.*

► Work with others. *Discussing topics with fellow students will further your understanding as it will give you exposure to a wider variety of views and ideas. Vocalizing your take on a topic will also be helpful. As you speak and try to formulate your thoughts on something, you realize where the gaps in your knowledge are and also put things into a logical order in your mind. Working with others is also a good discipline in that, if someone else is working hard, you will probably follow suit. Just make sure that you don't just casually meet up with friends for a coffee with the vague notion of doing some work. Here again, structure is important. If you plan what you are going to study as a group, you are far more likely to be successful. It is a good idea to go over past examination papers with a group of fellow students. Hearing how they would answer questions is often illuminating. Do not automatically assume that others will be right but consider their ideas alongside your own.*

▶ Keep attending tutorials. *This will keep you in touch with your tutor and with other students. You will find out what other students are up to and will also gather many useful tips from your tutor.*

Memory

Many students panic about exams not because they don't know their subject but because they are afraid that their memory will fail them. They fear that, under exam conditions and with the limited amount of time available, they will simply not be able to recall what they know.

Insight

Exams are not a test of memory but are meant to test your understanding of the course material. If there is something you do not understand or feel unsure of – even at the revision stage – don't hesitate to ask your tutors.

There are a number of tricks and tips you can use to overcome this fear and to improve your memory. Understanding how you learn will help to direct your revision more effectively so look back at the section on learning styles in Chapter 2. Help your memory along by trying the following:

▶ Planning – *it can't be said often enough, organized study is far more effective than a haphazard, untidy approach.*
▶ Keep what you have to commit to memory to a minimum – *condense your notes as much as possible.*
▶ Learn actively – *interact with your notes.*
▶ Understand what you're learning – *it is far easier to memorize something you understand than to learn by rote. If there are important parts of your course that you do not yet understand, you will be able to obtain help from your tutor if you do not leave it too late.*
▶ Use repetition – *go through the same subject matter in a number of different ways to help you to remember them. You might use different sources for the same information – notes, articles, your condensed notes and so on.*
▶ Use colour and illustration – *the more visual the material, the easier it is to remember it, so use different-coloured highlighters and pens, add little drawings if you're artistic, and underline or highlight the particularly important points in your condensed notes. You may find during the exam that a particular revision card or sheet of notes comes back to you because of the colour – you will visualize how it was written.*
▶ Make connections – *find links between the different parts of the subject that you are studying. Spider diagrams are useful for this – look back at the various ways to take notes discussed in Chapter 4. This is part of active learning and will help you to recall a lot of information at once.*
▶ Discuss the material with fellow students – *this will clarify your thoughts and help you to organize your knowledge. It may also show where you need to put in some further work.*
▶ Test yourself – *use previous exam papers or exam-type questions you have made up for yourself to give you useful practice in recalling what you know.*
▶ Try mnemonics – *these are devices used to help you remember important facts and some people find them really useful.*

A common mnemonic is using the first letters of a number of key words to make another word. This new word will then remind you of the original concept. If your tutors or fellow students have suggested any mnemonics, make a note of them and see if they are helpful to you.

▶ Consider what memory tricks you already use – *you might arrange words in a particular order, link words with mental images or use colour to help you remember* – and use them to full effect during your revision period.

Insight

The signs in the *Highway Code* have to be memorized in order to pass the theory test. This task can be made appreciably easier if you have practical experience of using these signs – so get out and about and take special note of the signs you see.

Quick revision test

1 *How can you be prepared for making the most of short periods of time becoming available during your revision period?*
2 *Give two ways in which practising answering exam questions is a useful revision technique.*
3 *Name three things you should get together when you are organizing your study materials at the start of your intensive revision period.*
4 *Name two passive methods of revision and two active methods.*
5 *How can you use index cards to good effect in your revision?*

10 THINGS TO REMEMBER

1 *Revision is not the time to learn something new – your exam preparation should concentrate on the materials you have already studied. It gives you the chance to pull the entire course together and to look at the bigger picture.*

2 *Reading materials repeatedly is not a good way to revise – an active approach is better. For example condense your notes, try a past exam paper, record yourself or work with others.*

3 *Start your revision as soon as possible. Try to keep it in mind from the beginning of your course; review your work regularly, make revision cards, plan revision periods into your study timetable and make brief, clear notes from the start.*

4 *When you start your revision in earnest make a plan; draw up a study timetable and organize course materials.*

5 *Useful revision activities include summarizing notes and handouts, practising with exam questions as well as 'normal life' activities such as sleep, work and family commitments plus some time for relaxation.*

6 *Review your course so that you know exactly what the most important topics are and then concentrate on these in your revision.*

7 *Take great care when selecting topics to revise. It is a mistake to leave out whole chunks of your course.*

8 *Prepare outlines from past exam questions and then produce essays. Time yourself so that you have plenty of practice at writing under exam conditions.*

9 *Keep attending tutorials right up to the end of the course – you will gather useful tips from your tutors and from other students.*

10 *Although exams are not really intended to be a test of memory, there are ways that you can help yourself to remember as you carry out your revision such as making links in the subject area you are studying or using colour to assist your memory.*

11

Exam preparation

In this chapter you will learn:
- *how to plan to pass your examinations*
- *how to write essays in exams*
- *about techniques that will be useful on the day.*

Plan to pass

Have you heard the saying 'failing to plan is planning to fail'? Good preparation and planning will help you just as much in passing examinations as in any other area of your life. In the case of exams, you must follow a structured revision schedule as discussed in the previous chapter and also plan the strategy that you will follow on the day.

As the exam day approaches and you are well into your revision, you should have found out all the basic information concerned with your exam. This will include:

▶ The exact dates and times of each exam. *Double-check these – it's not unknown for people to turn up on the wrong day for an exam.*

▶ Where the exams will be held. *Do you know how to get there? And how long it will take you? Note that the time your journey takes could vary according to the day of the week and the time of day. Allow yourself plenty of time. Arriving late can be disastrous – you could arrive stressed and not give your best performance or, worse still, you could be so late that you're refused entry.*

▶ The instructions you will be given. *These vary little from year to year so check out previous years' papers and make sure you understand them. They usually cover where to write your name and your identification number if you have one, how many questions you will have to answer, how long you're allowed, whether you can use rough paper for workings out and if you have to hand these rough notes in.*

Another aspect that might be covered here (and if it isn't then you need to find out the information for yourself, well ahead of the exam) is just what you are allowed to take with you into the exam room. Most exams ban books apart, perhaps, from a dictionary but your exam may be different. You may be allowed to take a calculator into the room plus a supply of pens and pencils. You may have to leave any bags and briefcases outside the exam room. Exam rules and conventions can vary widely, so make sure that you know exactly what instructions you must follow.

▶ The structure of the exam paper. *How many questions? Are they all allocated equal marks? Are they all essay questions? Or multiple-choice?*

▶ Exactly how you will be assessed. *Find out whether the exams will be marked internally or externally, will all the questions have equal marks allocated or are some questions more valuable than others?*

Another important part of your preparations should include staying positive. You must plan to pass and be convinced that you are perfectly capable of being successful. Of course, a small amount of worry about your result is normal and can even be helpful if it makes you work more effectively to ensure success. However, too much worry and negativity can be a definite drawback. Try not to build up the exam out of all proportion. As I've said before, it is not a life-threatening event. However, you definitely do want to pass this exam that you've put so much effort into, so you need to give it your best shot. As I said way back in Chapter 1, the essence of positive thinking is that you can achieve more if your thoughts are positive ones than if they are negative ones, and this is especially appropriate in exam preparation and performance. If you continually catch yourself saying 'If I fail ...', consciously change it to 'When I pass ...'

Use visualization techniques. Picturing yourself with that certificate or receiving your results envelope – with good pass marks, of course! – will help to build your confidence. Visualization can also be used to make taking the exam more comfortable and worry-free for you. Picture yourself walking into the exam room, seeing how it is set up and the invigilators waiting, then sitting down at a desk and listening carefully to the instructions you will be given. In your mind's eye, turn over the question paper. Now, do you know what you will do next? If not, this is where some planning has to be done. Make sure you know the following:

▶ *How long you will allow for each question?*
▶ *Will you start writing straight away or read through the paper and plan which questions you will answer? Some people need to find a question they like the look of and get writing immediately to settle their nerves, whereas others prefer to allocate a few minutes of their time to working out the questions to tackle.*
▶ *What sort of outlining technique will you use? Will it be in list form or a spider diagram or simply notes quickly jotted down? You should have practised this as part of your revision schedule.*

Visualizing this sort of scenario in this amount of detail can be very helpful in settling your nerves as it will feel familiar when you actually do it. It will also help to highlight where the deficiencies in your revision are.

Insight

Obtaining – and working on – as many past examination papers as you can should be an essential part of your revision and planning.

Writing essays in exams

Writing essays in exams is different from writing them for coursework – but there are many similarities too. Let's look first at the similarities:

- ▶ *You should start by analysing the question – check out the details of this in Chapter 8.*
- ▶ *They still need planning – look back to the section about essay outlines in Chapter 8.*
- ▶ *They should have a beginning, a middle and an end.*
- ▶ *You must stick to the point – do not attempt to write everything you know about the subject of the question. Adding irrelevant detail will not win you any marks. The examiner will have a schedule of marks to allocate. If you mention something that is not on this schedule, you will not get any extra marks for it.*
- ▶ *Most importantly – you should ensure that the essay answers the question.*

Now we can move on to the differences. These are important because they can make your task easier. Many of the areas of difference are caused by the fact that time is limited in exams. The examiners know that you can produce only a restricted amount of detail in the time allowed and that in the stressed circumstances of an exam most people will not be able to recall everything they know or to present the work in the way that they would under normal circumstances. Here are the main differences:

- ▶ *You will have far less time available. How many hours do you usually spend producing an essay as a course assignment? Two, three, five or even ten hours? No matter what sort of examination you're sitting, if you have to produce more than one essay you will not have anywhere near that amount of time. You may well have less than one hour. You will need to reduce all the processes that you usually go through when producing an essay – the planning, searching (in your mind) for material, producing an outline and writing – down into the 40 minutes or whatever time*

*you're allowed. Although there's so little time available, do not
be tempted to abandon the planning stage. Brainstorming and
preparing an outline will be time well spent because it will make
the writing easier – you won't run out of things to write and
you'll know just where you're going with your answer.*

▶ *You will write fewer words. There just isn't time to produce a
major work.*
▶ *You won't be able to include all the detail that you would use
if you were able to research the topic thoroughly and spend
more time on it.*
▶ *Your presentation is less important. As long as your writing
is legible, it will be OK – even if it does look a bit scruffy or
spidery!*
▶ *Minor errors in spelling and grammar are not usually penalized.*
▶ *You won't be able to include a bibliography.*
▶ *They will be far less polished than essays you've produced for
coursework – but that's fine; it's normal.*

Despite the constraints, you will be surprised by just how much
you can cram into the time you're allowed. Producing a winning
essay in an exam is as much about taking an organized approach as
it is about the actual writing. Later in this chapter we will look at
the practicalities of writing an essay under exam conditions.

Insight

Writing an essay longhand is something that you should
practise during your revision. You may have become unused
to writing by hand if all your work is usually typed straight
on to a computer.

The day before

It's certainly tempting to try to cram in as much revision as possible
on the day before your exam. You might get up early and go over
all your revision notes and cards and keep going, fuelled by plenty
of strong coffee and some junk food, until you can hardly keep

your eyes open, finally falling into bed in the early hours and then tossing and turning until the alarm goes off on the day of the exam. Don't. A far better approach is to do very little – even take the day off from studying if you possibly can. Most people, however, will need the reassurance of at least running quickly through their notes and checking a few final details. It's unlikely at this stage that very much will sink in so don't spend the whole day and evening revising. This will just result in your feeling tired and confused. Your time would be better spent relaxing. Check your details for tomorrow – exam location and time, getting your things together (pens, pencils, etc., plus the clothes you're going to wear) – so that on the day you will have as little as possible to worry about.

Try to relax the evening before and do not let that relaxation involve too much alcohol – that will just put you in danger of feeling groggy in the morning and that's no way to be on an exam day. Far better to get some fresh air and exercise or to do any activity that takes your mind off the forthcoming exam. Get to bed reasonably early the night before – have a relaxing bath before you do.

Insight

It is important not to become too stressed immediately before sitting an exam. A little stress can be beneficial but too much can cause you to panic. Try to plan some relaxation for the day before.

On the day

Even before you arrive at the examination centre there is plenty you can do to help yourself to pass the exam. Your aim should be to arrive in the peak of condition, in a calm state of mind, in plenty of time and fully equipped. Here's a checklist of what you can do:

▶ Eat breakfast. *A hungry body does not function at its peak so make sure you have a healthy breakfast before you leave home (and lunch, of course, if the exam is in the afternoon).*

- ▶ Relax. *If you find yourself with a bit of time before you have to leave home, you could perhaps meditate a little or listen to some soothing music.*
- ▶ Breathe deeply. *Practising a breathing exercise will only take a minute or two but will calm you down if you're starting to feel in a panic. Sit quietly and breathe in through your nose. Count the length of your in-breath. (Just breathe naturally. You might breathe in for a count of three, four, five or more – that's not important.) Then simply breathe out through your nose for the same count. Continue for five more breaths. Equalizing your breath in this way will mean that you're not thinking about anything else and you will very quickly relax.*
- ▶ Set off in plenty of time. *Rushing into the exam room at the last minute is not conducive to a calm start to the exam so allow time for traffic problems and so on. If you arrive early, try not to stand with friends indulging in mutual panic. Find a corner for yourself so that you can keep calm, or go off for a walk on your own.*

When you're finally in the exam room, seated at your desk, make sure you listen. The invigilator will probably read out some instructions – what you should do in the case of a fire (and yes, this does happen; it happened to me once!), what warning, if any, will be given when the exam is nearing its end, what you should do if you need anything such as extra writing paper, when you can start and what you should do if there are problems. The invigilator may also give you specific instructions about your question paper. Ignoring such instructions could mean the difference between pass and fail.

Insight

No matter how many exams you have previously taken, do not let yourself think that you know it all. Rules do change and different venues can come with different instructions, so it is essential to listen to any instructions you may be given immediately prior to an exam.

When you first turn over the question paper, you will probably feel nervous and not quite able to take in any detail, so it's a good idea to give the paper a quick skim through, noting questions that you think you might be able to do a good job on. As we said earlier, the structure of the exam should not be a surprise to you if you've done your research and checked out plenty of previous exam papers in advance. When you've settled down a bit – just a couple of minutes into the exam as there's no time to waste – it's a good idea to make a time plan so that you know what you should be doing and when. You need to make the very best use of the limited time you have in an exam and a timetable is the best way to keep track of time. With an exam time plan you will schedule in all the tasks you have to accomplish in the time allotted – reading the paper, choosing the questions, deciding the order in which you will answer them, the outlining and the writing.

Let's take an example based on a common exam format – with four essay-type questions to answer in three hours. You cannot just divide the three hours by four and then spend 45 minutes on each question as this will not allow you time to plan, to think and to check your answers at the end. So, how might your plan look?

2.00 p.m.	Read quickly through the paper, noting which questions you might attempt – a simple tick or asterisk on the exam paper next to the relevant questions will be sufficient.
2.10 p.m.	Brainstorm and outline the answer to the first question you have decided to attempt.
2.15 p.m.	Write your answer to the first question you are answering.
2.50 p.m.	Plan your answer to your second question.
2.55 p.m.	Write your answer to the second question you are answering.
3.30 p.m.	Plan your answer to your third question.
3.35 p.m.	Write your answer to the third question you are answering.
4.10 p.m.	Plan your answer to your fourth question.
4.15 p.m.	Write your answer to the fourth question you are answering.

| 4.50 p.m. | Check through your answers. |
| 5.00 p.m. | Hand in your paper. |

Of course, this is a *very* rough plan – it is highly unlikely that you will be able to keep to it precisely but it should guide you as to how much time you can spend on each task and prevent you from going seriously over on one question to the detriment of others. That is almost certainly the route to failure.

Next make your decision which question you're going to answer first. The sooner you can start writing, having given proper consideration to your question choice of course, the sooner you will lose your nerves a bit and start to gain marks. So, how do you make your question choice? Remember that the whole point of your being in the exam room is to pass and that the first marks you get for each question you attempt are the easiest to gain. You will – hopefully – cover the important basics in each of your answers and gain the bulk of your marks relatively easily. The extra detail in each topic will provide the additional marks that you need to get a good pass and these marks are harder to come by.

What you're looking for in making your question choice are those topics that you have revised and for which, therefore, you are confident of the basic, but important, information to include. Choose questions where you can get the easy marks. Do not let the wording of the questions put you off. You're looking for the topics you've revised so try to get to the nub of the question straight away. If it's about a topic you know little about – discard it. If, by the same token, it's about a topic that you know well, which figured prominently in your revision plans – perhaps some of the detail from your revision cards immediately springs to mind – then that is definitely a question you should attempt. The wording may be a little complicated but you can sort that out when you're analysing the question and brainstorming your answer.

You're now sitting in the exam room, question paper in front of you, your rough plan completed and you've found a question that you want to attempt. Let's look at your next moves – before you start writing:

▶ Look carefully at the question. *What is it actually asking you to do? It is often helpful to underline key words in the question. For example:*

'Freedom of speech is a right that we must all defend.' Discuss.

You may underline as follows:
*'<u>Freedom of speech</u> is a <u>right</u> that we must <u>**all defend**</u>.' **Discuss**.*

*Remember that, when the question says '**discuss**', it means that **you must examine the topic in detail** and then debate the argument (refer back to Chapter 8 for other important words you'll find in essay questions), so you'll need to know what is meant by 'freedom of speech' and 'right'. As we discussed earlier, it is sometimes helpful to rewrite the question for yourself – or at least to paraphrase it. This will help you to understand what the question requires.*

▶ Brainstorm what you know about the topic that will help you to answer the question. *Write down everything that is relevant and don't worry about writing it down in order or making it neat. Just get your ideas and the things you need to remember to include in your answer down on the rough paper without delay.*

▶ Now, take the results of your brainstorming session and use them to write an outline of your answer. *Remember the all-important beginning, middle and end. Decide how you will start your essay, then decide the order for the main points that you've jotted down that will form the main body. You may like to write a number next to each point indicating the order in which you will use them. Plan how you will end your answer by drawing all the important points together and reaching a conclusion.*

▶ Make sure you're going to answer the question. *Does your outline look like it's covered what will be needed in the answer? It's easy to go off at a tangent and write down all sorts of irrelevancies but you will know by now that you will*

get no marks if your answer does not answer the question.
You might have misread or misinterpreted the question, so read
it again now that you've got an outline – just as a last check.
▶ Keep calm, stay confident – *and then start writing.*

But what if you think you can't answer any of the questions? This
might be just as a result of stress. Take a deep breath and read
through the questions again. If you've revised well you should now
find that some ideas are springing into your mind. You will be
recalling a few points that you can put into some of your answers.
Jot them down. If you're still in a panic, choose just one question that
you at least understand the general gist of and start an outline for it.
Brainstorm everything you know about it as detailed above. This will
trigger off some ideas and by this time you will be on your way.

Some common exam mistakes

As you plan and write your answers, make sure that you are not
making one of the following common exam mistakes:

▶ *Not answering the question – this is one that examiners*
  always mention as being a reason for failure.
▶ *Not keeping to the point – don't go off at a tangent. The*
  things you're writing may be perfectly correct but if you've
  strayed from the point you won't get any marks for them.
▶ *Poor presentation – while you won't get too many marks for*
  a perfectly presented answer paper unless you've answered
  the questions properly, you should make things as easy for
  the marker as possible. This includes making sure that your
  writing is legible and using correct spelling, punctuation and
  starting paragraphs in the right places.
▶ *Giving a biased answer – you are expected to present a*
  balanced case, including arguments and evidence to support
  both sides of a case, especially if the question says 'discuss'
  or 'compare and contrast', so do not concentrate on only
  one view.

▶ *Not giving enough evidence to prove a point – you should not simply state a point and expect your reader to believe it, but must provide sufficient relevant evidence.*

▶ *Lack of time management – if you spend too much time on one question it will probably be to the detriment of other questions, so you must have a rough time plan in mind and stick to it as much as you can. An even worse thing to do is to produce a perfect – but time-consuming – answer to one question and then miss the answer to another one altogether because you've run out of time.*

And finally, checking

What are you checking for? Do you think 'Well, I've done my best I don't know any more about this subject. I just want to hand in this paper and get away. I never find any mistakes anyway'? You've allowed 10 minutes in your plan for this task and this is what you should be checking for:

▶ Have you answered the question? *This is the single most common reason for exam failure. Read again each question that you've answered and make sure the answer you've given matches up and does the job. If you find, at the last minute, that you've missed out some important pieces of information or argument, write them down at the end of your answer paper, making it clear which question they refer to.*

▶ Is the whole answer legible? *If there are any bits where you've rushed too much and your writing is unclear, cross it out and correct it.*

▶ Have you followed the instructions about numbering your questions and so on? *If not, this should be easy to put right.*

▶ Have you answered the correct number of questions? *This is a particularly easy mistake to make if you have to choose a certain number of questions from each of two or more sections of the exam paper.*

▶ Have you checked for spelling mistakes? *They're easy to make when we're under pressure.*

- Have you checked your punctuation? *A missed comma or full stop makes things more difficult to read and we don't want to make life difficult for the examiner, do we?*
- Does any more information spring to mind while you're reading through? *If so, add it to the end of your answer paper, again making it clear which question it refers to.*

Insight

Everyone makes mistakes so checking your answer paper is essential. Reading through the instructions on the question paper too may highlight something you've done wrong – not filling in your exam reference number or answering the wrong number of questions for example – and you will be able to put it right before you hand it in.

When you get to this point you should feel that you've done all you possibly can to pass this exam. Follow the instructions for handing in your answers and leaving the exam room, breathe a sigh of relief and then start celebrating!

A different exam – the driving theory test

Since 1996 everyone who wants to obtain a driving licence must sit an exam to prove they have knowledge of the *Highway Code* and the right attitude to safe driving. The driving theory test, which must be successfully negotiated before the practical test can be taken, can be just as nerve-wracking for the entrants as any other exam and is especially stressful because many of the people sitting it are not used to being in an exam situation.

The most commonly failed sections of the theory test regard documents and the rules of the road, and the main reason for these failures – as with any other type of exam – is insufficient or ineffective preparation. There is plenty of material available to help with this preparation – some material, in the form of a CD-ROM explaining the process of taking the theory test is sent to entrants along with their first theory test booking confirmation letter. Becoming familiar with this is obviously essential and is the equivalent of entrants of other types of exam becoming familiar with the instructions and format of past examination papers.

The driving theory test is split into two distinct parts:

▶ *A multiple-choice test of 35 questions.*
▶ *A hazard perception test of 14 video clips in which you have to identify 15 developing hazards.*

For the multiple-choice questions there are three books that form the source material:

▶ The Highway Code.
▶ Know Your Traffic Signs.
▶ *The* Driving Skills *series.*

Demonstration of complete familiarity with these source materials is necessary to obtain a pass. Other material can also be a tremendous help in the revision period prior to taking the test and this includes many books that are readily available or the complete set of theory test questions and answers can also be obtained in book format or on CD-ROM. Studying for the multiple-choice section of the theory test is mainly down to hard work and developing a memory bank of the road signs, etc., but taking driving lessons (and also taking notice when being driven about by other people) at the same time as studying for the theory test will be extremely helpful as the signs will become more meaningful and therefore easier to recall.

The hazard perception test requires just as much preparation and this can be helped by working with specially prepared materials supplied by the Driving Standards Agency (the DSA). A DVD or video can be obtained entitled *'The Official Guide to Hazard Perception'* that is designed for use with the guidance of a professional trainer. It adopts a modular, structured approach to identifying hazards and includes:

▶ *looking for clues*
▶ *scanning and planning*

- *prioritizing*
- *responding to hazards*
- *risk reduction*
- *use of the 'mirror, signal, manoeuvre' routine*
- *example video clips of hazards.*

Again, hazard perception can be learned using the recommended materials but will be made easier with practical driving experience.

As with any other learning task, preparing for the driving theory test takes plenty of effort and will be greatly helped by actively engaging with the topic. Although the temptation is to simply learn the traffic signs and so on by rote, make sure that you do not take an exclusively passive approach. Get out there and see the signs you're trying to learn. See them in use and think about what they mean to drivers, what action you are expected to take when you see it and whether it is a command or simply there for your guidance. Think about the signs and their meanings and actively use them and this will ensure that you remember them in that all-important test.

Quick revision test

1 Give three similarities and two differences between writing essays under exam conditions and writing them as assignments.
2 Name three things (apart from turning up!) that you need to do on the day of the exam.
3 When planning your timetable for an exam, why shouldn't you just divide the time allowed by the number of questions to be answered?
4 List three things that you should check your answer paper for at the end of an exam.
5 What are the two distinct parts of the driving theory test?

10 THINGS TO REMEMBER

1   As part of your revision, make sure that you find out all the basic information about the exam – including dates, times, venue, exam instructions and structure.

2   Plan how you will tackle the exam paper. Visualization techniques and positive thinking can help you to pass the exam and to cope with exam stress.

3   Writing essays in exams is different to writing for coursework – there will be less time available and presentation will not matter as much. However, you still need to produce an essay that answers the question.

4   Try to relax a little on the day before sitting an exam.

5   Set off in plenty of time to reach the exam venue – and make sure you take everything you need with you.

6   It's a good idea to make an exam time plan so that you know how long you can spend on each answer. Remember to allow yourself time for checking at the end too.

7   The most important thing about answering an exam question is answering the actual question you have been asked and don't go off on a tangent. Make sure you have used sufficient evidence to support your argument and that your presentation is acceptable.

8   Keep an eye on the time during the exam. Spending too much time on one question can leave you with insufficient time to do yourself justice on other questions.

9   Always check your answer paper before handing it in.

10 If you are sitting a driving theory test make sure that you have prepared well and have used the materials sent to you with your test confirmation letter – you should aim to become familiar with the format of the test.

12

Where to next?

In this chapter you will learn:
- *what to do and what not to do when the exams are over*
- *about the choices and decisions to be made*
- *where to look for help and advice.*

Introduction

When you have finished taking your exams, you may feel a bit lost. This can happen to people who pass as well as those who fail. Sometimes it is not about your future plans but about coming to the end of a difficult and intense period of your life. The sudden cessation of what has become a major part of your life – revising for exams – can cause you to wonder what to do with yourself. There will be a big gap in your life. But life will go on and you will need to make some decisions about your future at this stage regardless of whether you have passed or failed your exams.

Pass or fail?

However you feel after the exam has finished – elated, confident, disappointed, fearful, hopeful – try not to worry. The exam is over now and you cannot affect the result – it is all now in the hands of the examiners. You can do no more.

One scenario that almost always follows an exam is the post-mortem. This is where you meet up with fellow students and go through the paper question by question. Try not to get involved in this. As we've said, the exam is over now so it's too late to do anything about it. Inevitably, the post-exam discussion will throw up some people saying how easy they found it (putting fear into you that you've done it all wrong) or other people saying it was impossible and that nobody could have passed such an exam. Taking notice of either of these viewpoints will do you no good. Neither will make you feel better and, of course, other people's views of the paper are irrelevant.

All that's left for you to do now is to celebrate the end of a difficult, intense period, take it easy and wait for the results to drop through your letterbox. In the meantime, do not panic. It is impossible to be 100 per cent sure of your result so patience is required now.

If the results arrive and you've obtained a good pass, congratulations! You will need to plan your next move carefully, so look at the later section in this chapter entitled 'Moving on'.

If, on the other hand, you get results that are not satisfactory, you will need to consider whether you will be able to do a resit, to repeat the year or even if you will be able to appeal against the marking decisions. Incorrect marks are very occasionally given, but it is unusual because marking goes through a number of checking procedures to ensure fairness and accuracy. Mistakes do happen, however, so you should consult your tutors immediately if you think you may be the victim of a marking error. Your tutors will, if they are in agreement, arrange for an official complaint to be sent to the examiners.

It is far more likely that, in the event of a failed exam, you will need to resit the exam or even repeat the whole year. Remember that there is no compulsion about this and what you do at this stage should be a decision you will take with the help of your tutors and possibly counsellors from your college. There may also be financial implications of your failure – will you be able to afford to repeat the year? Again, consulting the experts will help. Your college tutors and counsellors will be the best people to help you with this dilemma.

Above all, try to keep things in perspective. It is only a failed exam and there are always choices that can be made and solutions to be found.

Sources of information and support

If you have questions following the receipt of your exam results – whether you've passed or failed – the first people to approach are almost always those concerned with running your course. This may be your tutor or a counsellor, depending on the situation you find yourself in. They will probably have dealt with questions similar to yours many, many times and will usually have the information you need readily available or will be able to point you in the right direction. There may also be a careers counsellor in your college who will be able to advise you as to what your choices are at this point. Do not ignore this sort of assistance. It is there because students always have questions and need help to find the best solutions to their problems and to find the best sources of information.

If the exam you have just passed was the end of your course, you may be wondering just where you go next (although deciding this is usually a process best carried out alongside studying in your final year rather than leaving it until the very end of your course). Most colleges and universities have specialists who can help you to plan your personal development and you should take full advantage of this. In the next section we will look at how you can plan your future career.

Don't forget also that you may get help and support from your family and friends. Just talking about a problem can sometimes help you to see the way through it.

There are also lots of sources of support online – check out the useful website section at the end of this chapter.

Moving on

The majority of people who study and sit exams do so to further their career prospects. If this is you, then you will need to continue your career planning following your exam results. As with any other sort of plan, a career plan will need to set out your goals and give you strategies for making progress towards them. After a major milestone such as finishing a set of exams – and perhaps achieving an important qualification – your career plan will need to be reviewed and brought up to date. If you have passed your exam, perhaps you will simply go on to the next phase of your plan, but it is still worthwhile reviewing whether your goals continue to be right for you and to remind yourself of where you are heading. If, however, you have failed your exam, you will definitely need to review your plans for the future. It may be that you will simply need to delay your plans while you take a resit or repeat the year.

More seriously, your exam result may mean that you have to shift direction. Of course, career planning does not just involve passing exams and moving on to the next course of study. There are many elements to a comprehensive plan that will lead to the well-rounded, well-qualified and experienced individual to impress prospective employers. Your plan should cover things such as employment experience, skills that you have, or will acquire, volunteer work and evidence that you can take responsibility, in addition to your qualifications. In short, you need to build up a portfolio of evidence of skills and attributes that an employer will value. You must start looking at how you will appear to an employer and then make a plan that will improve you as a whole. Most employers will be looking for:

▶ Good exam results *in appropriate subjects.*
▶ Work experience. *While any work experience is better than*

none (even bar or shop work shows that you are capable of turning up regularly for work), you should try to get some work that will show other skills. Maybe you can get some holiday work in the area in which you aim to work when you have finished studying. In this case, you will not only get the chance to see if it is for you but also it will be a valuable addition to your CV and may impress prospective employers.

▶ Volunteer experience. *This is always valued by employers and can be a unique experience for anyone – a lot can be learned.*

▶ Evidence of skills acquisition. *To decide what skills you need to acquire and to demonstrate on a CV, you need to think like an employer. You're looking for things that will make you stand out from other applicants. Perhaps you've funded your own studies (good money-management skills, resourcefulness) or have been involved in a project that took up a lot of your time and helped people less fortunate than yourself (commitment, selflessness, altruism) or have nursed a member of your family through illness (caring skills, commitment).*

If you feel that you have shortfalls in any of these areas, then your career plan will need to address them. You may need to improve the quality of your work experience and plan to apply for some interesting holiday work for your next break or to check out the volunteer opportunities that are available to you.

The careers advisory services attached to your college will have enormous resources available about careers and how to prepare for them. They will be able to advise the details of prospective employers and the training programmes that may be on offer. But more than this, they will be able to talk to you to discover your aims and ambitions and then help you to match these to what you can achieve and how to go about it. They can advise on subject options, know what the competition is like for the more popular job areas and will have close connections with many of the larger employers. In short, they can help you to make a career plan or, if you already have one, to refine it so that you continue to make progress towards your goals.

If you are preparing or updating your career plan, you can now see that if you concentrate solely on obtaining qualifications you will not have sufficient to interest an employer and to set yourself apart from other applicants. Your plan should include writing a CV and keeping it up to date. Imagine yourself discussing this CV with potential employers. This might highlight your shortfalls if you realize that you have very little to discuss. While updating (or starting to write) your CV, don't forget to include the study skills you will have learned while working your way through this book and your course. If at first you think 'Well, there won't be much call for exam revision skills in the business world!' then think again. What about the analytical skills you've developed (reading to learn), the ability to express yourself succinctly (note taking), coping under pressure (sitting an exam) or goal setting and planning (organizing your study schedule)?

There are always opportunities to develop yourself and you should take advantage of as many of these as you possibly can. It will not be wasted time.

If you are now coming to the end of a course of study, you will probably have realized that it is just the end of one phase of your life and you will now be moving on to another phase with your goals in mind. You will also have realized that learning never ends. To keep progressing in your career, your education and in life in general, you will need to continue to develop in all sorts of ways and the study skills you have learned by working through this book will stand you in good stead.

Getting help if you have problems

As we all know, things do not always go smoothly. If you have been suffering high levels of stress during your course of study, you may need to get help to deal with it so that it does not affect you seriously in the future. Counsellors will be available to you at your college and you should take full advantage of the services they offer. They will be able to give you in-depth advice about how to deal with stress in all areas of your life, with a particular emphasis on how it affects your studies. If you are a mature student, perhaps studying independently, then your GP should be your first port of call if you feel that you are suffering unduly from stress. A certain amount of stress is, of course, normal, especially when studying and dealing with the additional strain of exams. But if the stress affects your sleep patterns or makes you feel unable to cope with normal life then you must get help.

It may be that you need to completely reorganize your plans and you will find that, immediately following exams, there will be plenty of help available. Colleges are usually geared up to help students – whether they have passed or failed – to decide on their next move.

Being a student can be a lonely experience and your problems will not get better if you hide away and ignore them. Whether you have study-related problems, stress, financial or health problems, you can be sure that the counsellors in your college will have seen and dealt with your problem before. They will know what resources are available to you and will point you in the right direction.

Financial problems are very common among students. Again, counsellors will be able to help and you could also approach the Citizens' Advice Bureau for assistance in managing your debt. As with other problems, getting help early is really important so don't delay – things will only get worse while you sit worrying about debt and not really tackling the problem.

When you're seeking help with a problem, no matter what the nature of the difficulty you are having, and regardless of whom you are approaching for help, whether it be your tutor, a counsellor, a careers advisor, your GP or someone from an outside body such as the Citizens' Advice Bureau, you will help yourself to get a better result if you prepare for the meeting. As in any other area, you should plan ahead. Try to accumulate evidence and background to your problem such as:

- ▶ *A note of what you think your problem is.*
- ▶ *What you've already tried.*
- ▶ *Details of your exam results if these are part of the problem – solid information, rather than just stating 'I've failed', will be an invaluable aid to the person helping you.*
- ▶ *Up-to-date figures of all your incomings and outgoings if your problem is about your finances.*

Whatever sort of problem you encounter during your studies, you should try to work through it. However, if it starts to affect your everyday life then you should get help – it will always be available and you just need to have the confidence to seek it out.

Special problems

If you find that things that you've had to cope with throughout your life are getting in the way of your studies – maybe you have dyslexia, a physical challenge or difficulties with reading, writing or numbers – there will be help available. There are lots of examples of people who have achieved success despite their drawbacks or disadvantages, so don't let anything stand in your way. It is often the case that people who have experienced difficulties during their school years return to education later and need a bit of help. They may have been judged harshly at school and then ignored and their problems not explored and resolved, or their disadvantages may have caused a lack of continuity in their education. Sometimes it is not possible to catch up at the time but then, many years later, lots of people come back to education with a new determination. For these people there is plenty of help and support.

If you have basic literacy or numeracy difficulties, the sooner you get some assistance the better. Many local colleges offer free classes to help to improve basic skills that will enhance not just your exam chances or career prospects but will help in many other areas of your life. If you're employed, try asking your employer for help with literacy and numeracy skills as there are plenty of programmes available that they can give you information about.

Up to 10 per cent of the UK population have dyslexia, with around 2 million people in the UK severely affected, but in years gone by the problem was not as well recognized as it is today so a lot of children had dyslexia that affected their educational development but were not given any help. Things have now, thankfully, changed and help is available from various sources. Try getting in touch with the British Dyslexia Association or the Dyslexia Institute (full details at the end of the chapter).

Likewise, there is specialist help available for other barriers to education such as physical challenges, lack of childcare facilities or being a single parent – you just have to go out and find the help and use it, together with your determination, to improve your circumstances. Check out the section on 'Useful websites and organizations' at the end of this book.

Answers to quick tests

Chapter 1

1 *Note taking, reading, writing essays and reports, planning, revising for examinations, sitting examinations.*
2 *Expected learning outcomes.*
3 *You can achieve more if your thoughts are positive ones than if they are negative ones.*
4 *Facing the fear.*
5 *To make them easier to deal with.*

Chapter 2

1 *A writing surface, a bookshelf, room for a computer, suitable lighting and a chair at the correct height.*
2 *Back up your files.*
3 *Never rewrite notes, stay focused, keep notes brief and tidy, and develop an effective filing system.*
4 *Visual, auditory and kinaesthetic.*
5 *Irritability, insomnia, eating, smoking or drinking too much, spending all your time studying, thinking that everyone is doing better than you, clumsiness, feeling sick at the thought of an assignment.*

Chapter 3

1 *Gaining a general understanding of the subject and some background knowledge.*
2 *Ignore them.*

3 *Your finger or a sheet of paper.*
4 *No. Some things, such as detailed instructions or texts that you have to closely analyse will require slower, more concentrated reading.*
5 *The contents page and the back cover blurb.*

Chapter 4

1 *To aid memory, to help to assimilate and understand information.*
2 *To gain information to write an essay, for exam revision, to help to understand a complicated piece of text.*
3 *Whether there are any handouts, your own way of working, whether you 'wander off' during lectures.*
4 *In the centre – like the spider's body.*
5 *Passive – reading them. Active – condensing them, recording the key words, using for another purpose such as writing mock-exam answers.*

Chapter 5

1 *A line of reasoning, a case being made, a point of view and a position being taken.*
2 *Evidence and examples.*
3 *At the end of the essay. You should highlight it or underline it and then decide if it is valid.*
4 *A clear conclusion.*
5 *Decide on your main argument, gather evidence, consider other points of view, reach a clear conclusion and review thoroughly.*

Chapter 6

1 Primary resources – *original documentation, your own data and observation, case studies, and original materials.* Secondary resources – *academic texts, books and articles and other people's data.*
2 *You are not allowed to take books from the reference section out on loan.*
3 *Library references by subject area.*
4 *A short summary.*
5 *'ac'.*

Chapter 7

1 *To aid comprehension.*
2 *Two negative words in a sentence will not express what is meant, as they will cancel one another out.*
3 *To show possession and to show where letters are missing.*
4 *Rewrite the question, gather information, outline the essay or report, etc., and then write.*
5 *A small number of categories would be better for using a line diagram.*

Chapter 8

1 *Contents page, summary, introduction, details of the research methodology, the report's findings, the conclusion, recommendations and appendices.*
2 *At the end.*

3 *They will save you time, potential pitfalls, and possible embarrassment during your presentation if your writing is not straight.*

4 *Tick off items on your schedule and reward yourself when you reach each milestone.*

5 *Decide your case, find arguments and search for evidence for and against these arguments.*

Chapter 9

1 *Creating a new document.*
2 *Header and Footer.*
3 *By facilitating online support groups and regular communication with tutors and fellow students.*
4 *A VLE is a system provided by a college that enables students to use learning materials and also to access details and facilities such as individual progress, bulletin boards, reminders, tracking tools and conferencing facilities.*
5 *Advantage – flexibility; disadvantage – discipline needed.*

Chapter 10

1 *Always carry some work around with you.*
2 *First, it gives confidence as you become familiar with both the exam format and the subject matter of the course and, second, active revision deepens understanding of course materials.*
3 *Your course overview, past exam papers, course books and articles, your notes, handouts plus all your files and loose papers.*
4 Passive – *rereading notes and copying out material.*
Active – *condensing notes and practising essay questions.*

5 *From prepared A4 sheets of important facts you can condense the material until you can get the really important information about that topic on to an index card to carry about with you and use when you have a few minutes to spare during the day.*

Chapter 11

1 Similarities – *you analyse the question in the same way, plan your answer by doing an outline, they both have a beginning, a middle and an end, you have to stick to the point and you must answer the question.* Differences – *in an exam there is less time available, you write fewer words, use less detail, do less research and presentation is not as important.*
2 *Eat, relax and set off in plenty of time.*
3 *This will not allow you time to plan, to think and to check your answers at the end.*
4 *That you have answered the question, the whole answer is legible, you have followed the instructions and answered the correct number of questions. Also check for spelling mistakes, punctuation errors. Finally, does any more information spring to mind while you're reading through?*
5 *A multiple-choice test and a hazard perception test.*

Taking it Further

Useful websites and organizations

British Dyslexia Association (BDA) – www.bdadyslexia.org.uk;
98 London Road, Reading RG1 5AU; Helpline 0118 966 8271;
Tel 0118 966 2677

Citizens' Advice Bureau – www.citizensadvice.org.uk

General advice for students – www.studentuk.uk.com

National Education Association (USA) – www.nea.org

Plenty of information to help you during your studies –
www.support4learning.org.uk

Learn Direct – www.learndirect.co.uk; Tel 0800 101 901.
Careers advice and advice about courses.

National Association of Volunteer Bureaux – www.navb.org.uk

National Literacy Trust – www.literacytrust.org.uk

American Literacy Council – www.americanliteracy.com

The Dyslexia Institute – www.dyslexia-inst.org.uk

The Lone Parent Support Group – www.lone-parents.org.uk

The Open University – www.open.ac.uk

UCAS (University and Colleges Admissions Service) – www.ucas.com

UK Government – www.direct.gov.uk. Contains many useful links and contacts.

UK Volunteer Opportunities – www.do-it.org.uk. Find one near you by simply entering your postcode.

If you are in the USA you can search for more information via the following search engines:
www.bing.com
www.google.com
www.lycos.com

Further reading

Bavister, S. and Vickers, A. (2004) *Teach Yourself Neuro-Linguistic Programming*, Hodder & Stoughton

McKenna, P. (2004) *Change Your Life in Seven Days*, Bantam

Wilding C. and Palmer, S. (2005) *Moody to Mellow*, Hodder Arnold

Wilkinson, G. (1997) *Understanding Stress*, British Medical Association

Index

Locators in *bold italics* refer to figures/diagrams. Locators for headings which also have subheadings refer to general aspects of the topic

LB
10419
W35
2010